# The Ordinary Pra[y]

# Traditional Lat[in] M[ass]

## (Extraordinary Form or *Vetus Ordo*)

# Benediction, Angelus

## and other prayers and devotions

Compiled by Joseph Shaw

## The Latin Mass Society

Cover picture: High Mass, celebrated by Fr Anthony Conlon, in the Chapel of Milton Manor House in Oxfordshire. Used with permission.

Translation by RPD.
Typsetting of chant by the Society of St Bede.
Illustrations by Stefano Mazzeo.

*Nihil obstat* TERRY TASTARD (Censor)

*Imprimatur* + VINCENT NICHOLS Cardinal Archbishop of Westminster

Date: 25th March 2015, The Annunciation of the Lord

The *Nihil obstat* and *Imprimatur* are a declaration that a book or pamphlet is considered to be free from doctrinal or moral error. It is not implied that those who granted the *Nihil obstat* or *Imprimatur* agree with the contents, opinion or statements expressed.

The Latin Mass Society
11–13 Macklin Street
London WC2B 5NH
www.lms.org.uk
Copyright © The Latin Mass Society, UK 2015
ISBN: 978-0-9932140-0-4
A catalogue record is available for this book from the British Library.
Printed by Intercity Communications Ltd, London UK .

# ABOUT THIS BOOKLET

The purpose of this booklet is to assist the Faithful to follow the Traditional Latin Mass, the Extraordinary Form or *Vetus Ordo,* as they are likely to find it celebrated in England and Wales today.

Since such help is particularly necessary at special events such as great feasts and pilgrimages, we have included variations not only for Sundays, weekdays, and the liturgical seasons, but for High and Pontifical Mass. The booklet does not contain the variations found with Masses for the Dead, Ember Days, or other special ceremonies such as those celebrated in the Easter Triduum, or Pontifical Low Mass.

A separate booklet for Masses for the Dead is in preparation.

This booklet strives to be in conformity with the Order of Mass as authorised in 1962, the *Manual of Prayers* authorised by the English Hierarchy in 1953, and the *Ritus Servandus* of 1954. The English translation of the Ordinary Prayers of the Mass has been newly prepared for this booklet, and follows the Douai-Rheims Bible, as revised by Bishop Challoner, where applicable.

This booklet should not be regarded as a definite guide to the rubrics, or as deprecating legitimate local practices. This is particularly so in the postures of the Faithful during Mass, for which no binding rules exist.

Similarly, the order of Benediction represents typical but by no means universal or binding practice.

We have included Latin versions of prayers where possible even when these are commonly said in the vernacular, as a matter of devotional and historical interest.

*Ut in omnibus glorificetur Deus.*

# ORDO MISSÆ

## Initium Missæ

*Turn to p.42* *for the* *'Asperges'* *or Vidi* *Aquam',* *which takes* *place before* *the principal* *Mass on* *Sundays.*

*Sacerdos:* In nómine Patris, ✠ et Fílii, et Spíritus Sancti. Amen.

Introíbo ad altáre Dei.

*Ministri:* Ad Deum, qui lætíficat iuventútem meam.

*S:* Iúdica me, Deus, et discérne causam meam de gente non sancta: ab hómine iníquo et dolóso érue me.

*M:* Quia tu es, Deus, fortitúdo mea: quare me repulísti, et quare tristis incédo, dum afflígit me inimícus?

*S:* Emítte lucem tuam et veritátem tuam: ipsa me deduxérunt, et adduxérunt in montem sanctum tuum, et in tabernácula tua.

*M:* Et introíbo ad altáre Dei: ad Deum, qui lætíficat iuventútem meam.

*S:* Confitébor tibi in cíthara, Deus, Deus meus: quare tristis es, ánima mea, et quare contúrbas me?

*M:* Spera in Deo, quóniam adhuc confitébor illi: salutáre vultus mei, et Deus meus.

*S:* Glória Patri, et Fílio, et Spirítui Sancto.

*M:* Sicut erat in princípio, et nunc, et semper: et in sǽcula sæculórum. Amen.

*S:* Introíbo ad altáre Dei.

*M:* Ad Deum, qui lætíficat iuventútem meam.

*S:* Adiutórium nostrum ✠ in nómine Dómini.

*M:* Qui fecit cælum et terram.

*S:* Confíteor Deo omnipoténti, beátæ Maríæ semper Vírgini, beáto Michaéli Archángelo, beáto Ioánni Bap-

# THE ORDER OF MASS

## Prayers at the Foot of the Altar

*Priest:* In the name of the Father, ✠ and of the Son, and of the Holy Ghost. Amen.

I will go in to the altar of God.

*Ministers:* To God who gives joy to my youth.

*P:* Judge me, O God, and distinguish my cause from the nation that is not holy: deliver me from the unjust and deceitful man.

*M:* For thou, O God, art my strength: why hast thou cast me off? and why do I go sorrowful whilst the enemy afflicts me?

*P:* Send forth thy light and thy truth: they have conducted me and brought me unto thy holy hill, even into thy tabernacles.

*M:* And I will go in to the altar of God, to God, who gives joy to my youth.

*P:* To thee, O God my God, I will give praise upon the harp: why art thou sad, O my soul? and why dost thou disquiet me?

*M:* Hope in God, for I will still give praise to him: the salvation of my countenance, and my God.

*P:* Glory be to the Father and to the Son and to the Holy Ghost.

*M:* As it was in the beginning, is now and ever shall be, world without end. Amen.

*P:* I will go in to the altar of God.

*M:* To God who gives joy to my youth.

*P:* Our help ✠ is in the name of the Lord

*M:* Who made heaven and earth.

*P:* I confess to almighty God, to blessed Mary ever-Virgin, to blessed Michael the Archangel, to blessed

Commonly used postures for the Faithful: **Kneel when the server kneels.**

*The 'Prayers at the Foot of the Altar', with the Psalm Iudica, are said at the bottom of the steps leading up to the Altar.*

*The Priest's Confiteor*

tístæ, sanctis Apóstolis Petro et Paulo, omnibus Sanctis, et vobis, fratres, quia peccávi nimis cogitatióne, verbo et ópere: mea culpa, mea culpa, mea máxima culpa. Ideo precor beátam Maríam semper Vírginem, beátum Michaélem Archángelum, beátum Ioánnem Baptístam, sanctos Apóstolos Petrum et Paulum, omnes Sanctos, et vos, fratres, oráre pro me ad Dóminum, Deum nostrum.

*M:* Misereátur tui omnípotens Deus, et, dimíssis peccátis tuis, perdúcat te ad vitam ætérnam.

*S:* Amen.

*The Server's Confiteor*

*M:* Confíteor Deo omnipoténti, beátæ Maríæ semper Vírgini, beáto Michaéli Archángelo, beáto Ioánni Baptístæ, sanctis Apóstolis Petro et Paulo, omnibus Sanctis, et tibi, Pater, quia peccávi nimis cogitatióne, verbo et ópere: mea culpa, mea culpa, mea máxima culpa. Ideo precor beátam Maríam semper Vírginem, beátum Michaélem Archángelum, beátum Ioánnem Baptístam, sanctos Apóstolos Petrum et Paulum, omnes Sanctos, et te, Pater, oráre pro me ad Dóminum, Deum nostrum.

*S:* Misereátur vestri omnípotens Deus, et, dimíssis peccátis vestris, perdúcat vos ad vitam ætérnam.

*M:* Amen.

*S:* Indulgéntiam, ✠ absolutiónem, et remissiónem peccatórum nostrórum tríbuat nobis omnípotens et miséricors Dóminus.

*M:* Amen.

*S:* Deus, tu convérsus vivificábis nos.

*M:* Et plebs tua lætábitur in te.

*S:* Osténde nobis, Dómine, misericórdiam tuam.

*M:* Et salutáre tuum da nobis.

*S:* Dómine, exáudi oratiónem meam.

*M:* Et clamor meus ad te véniat.

*S:* Dóminus vobíscum

*M:* Et cum spíritu tuo.

John the Baptist, to the holy Apostles Peter and Paul, to all the Saints, and to you, brothers, that I have sinned exceedingly in thought, word and deed, through my fault, through my fault, through my most grievous fault. Therefore I beseech blessed Mary ever-Virgin, blessed Michael the Archangel, blessed John the Baptist, the holy Apostles Peter and Paul, all the saints, and you, brothers, to pray for me to the Lord our God.

*M:* May almighty God have mercy on thee, and lead thee, with thy sins forgiven, to eternal life.

*P:* Amen.

*M:* I confess to almighty God, to blessed Mary ever-Virgin, to blessed Michael the Archangel, to blessed John the Baptist, to the holy Apostles Peter and Paul, to all the Saints, and to thee, Father, that I have sinned exceedingly in thought, word and deed, through my fault, through my fault, through my most grievous fault. Therefore I beseech blessed Mary ever-Virgin, blessed Michael the archangel, blessed John the Baptist, the holy apostles Peter and Paul, all the saints, and thee, Father, to pray for me to the Lord our God.

*P:* May almighty God have mercy on you, and lead you, with your sins forgiven, to eternal life.

*M:* Amen.

*P:* May the almighty and merciful Lord grant us pardon, ✠ absolution and remission of our sins.

*M:* Amen.

*P:* Thou wilt turn, O God, and bring us to life.

*M:* And thy people shall rejoice in thee.

*P:* Show us, O Lord, thy mercy.

*M:* And grant us thy salvation.

*P:* O Lord, hear my prayer.

*M:* And let my cry come unto thee.

*P:* The Lord be with you.

*M:* And with thy spirit.

S: Orémus. Aufer a nobis, quǽsumus, Dómine, iniquitátes nostras: ut ad Sancta sanctórum puris mereámur méntibus introíre. Per Christum Dóminum nostrum. Amen.

Oramus te, Dómine, per mérita Sanctórum tuórum, quorum relíquiæ hic sunt, et ómnium Sanctórum: ut indulgére dignéris ómnia peccáta mea. Amen.

*Blessing of incense at Sung and High Mass*

S: Ab illo benedicáris, in cuius honóre cremáberis. Amen.

# MISSA CATECHUMENORUM

## Introit: see Propers

*The two most common Chant Kyries for Sundays are found on p60 & 62.*

S: Kyrie, eléison.
M: Kyrie, eléison.
S: Kyrie, eléison.
M: Christe, eléison.
S: Christe, eléison.
M: Christe, eléison.
S: Kyrie, eléison.
M: Kyrie, eléison.
S: Kyrie, eléison.

*The Gloria is not always said on weekdays, and on Sundays is not said in Advent and between Septuagesima and Easter.*

S: Gloria in excélsis Deo.
S/Chorus: Et in terra pax homínibus bonæ voluntátis. Laudámus te. Benedícimus te. Adorámus te. Glorificámus te. Grátias ágimus tibi propter magnam glóriam tuam. Dómine Deus, Rex cæléstis, Deus Pater omnípotens.

Dómine Fili unigénite, Iesu Christe. Dómine Deus, Agnus Dei, Fílius Patris. Qui tollis peccáta mundi, miserére nobis. Qui tollis peccáta mundi, súscipe deprecatiónem nostram. Qui sedes ad déxteram Patris, miserére nobis. Quóniam tu solus Sanctus. Tu solus Dóminus. Tu solus Altíssimus, Iesu Christe.

Cum Sancto Spiritu ✠ in gloria Dei Patris. Amen.

*P:* Let us pray. Take away from us our iniquities, we pray, O Lord, that with pure minds we may worthily go in to the holy of holies. Through Christ our Lord. Amen.

We beseech thee, O Lord, by the merits of thy saints, whose relics are here, and of all the saints, that thou wouldst be pleased to forgive me all my sins. Amen.

*The Priest ascends to the Altar, and kisses it.*

*P:* Be thou blessed by Him in whose honour thou shalt be burned. Amen.

# THE MASS OF CATECHUMENS

*P:* Lord, have mercy.
*M:* Lord, have mercy.
*P:* Lord, have mercy.
*M:* Christ, have mercy.
*P:* Christ, have mercy.
*M:* Christ, have mercy.
*P:* Lord, have mercy.
*M:* Lord, have mercy.
*P:* Lord, have mercy.

**At Low Mass, remain kneeling. At Sung Masses, stand. Sit if the Priest sits.**

*P:* Glory to God in the highest,

*P/Choir:* And on earth peace to men of good will. We praise thee. We bless thee. We adore thee. We glorify thee. We give thee thanks for thy great glory. Lord God, heavenly King, O God almighty Father.

Lord Jesus Christ, Only Begotten Son. Lord God, Lamb of God, Son of the Father; who takest away the sins of the world, have mercy on us; who takest away the sins of the world, receive our prayer; who sittest at the right hand of the Father, have mercy on us. For thou alone art the Holy One. Thou alone art the Lord. Thou alone art the Most High, Jesus Christ,

With the Holy Ghost, ✠ in the glory of God the Father. Amen.

*S:* Dóminus vobíscum.
*M:* Et cum spíritu tuo.
*S:* Oremus.

## Collect: see Propers

*M:* Amen

## Epistle: see Propers

*M:* Deo grátias.

## Gradual, Alleluia, &c.: see Propers

*S/Diaconus:* Munda cor meum, ac lábia mea, omnípotens Deus, qui lábia Isaíæ prophétæ cálculo mundásti igníto: ita me tua grata miseratióne dignáre mundáre, ut sanctum Evangélium tuum digne váleam nuntiáre. Per Christum Dóminum nostrum. Amen.
*S/D:* Iube, domne (*vel* Dómine), benedícere.
*P:* Dóminus sit in corde tuo (meo) et in lábiis tuis (meis): ut digne et competénter annúnties (annúntiem) Evangélium suum.

*At High Mass:*
In nómine Patris, et Fílii, ✠ et Spíritus Sancti. Amen.

*S/D:* Dóminus vobíscum.
*M:* Et cum spíritu tuo.
*S/D:* Inítium (*vel* Sequéntia) sancti Evangélii secúndum N...
*M:* Glória tibi, Dómine.

## Gospel: see Propers

*M:* Laus tibi, Christe.

Collect & Gospel

*P:* The Lord be with you.
*R:*  And with thy spirit.
*P:* Let us pray.

*M:* Amen.

*M:* Thanks be to God.

**Sit for the Epistle.**

*At High Mass, the Epistle is sung by the Subdeacon, and the Gospel by the Deacon.*

*P/Deacon.* Cleanse my heart and my lips, almighty God, who didst cleanse the lips of the prophet Isaias with a burning coal: be pleased by thy gracious mercy so to cleanse me that I may worthily proclaim thy holy Gospel. Through Christ our Lord. Amen.
*P/D:* Pray, sir (*or* Lord), a blessing.
*P:* May the Lord be in thy (my) heart and on thy (my) lips, that thou mayst (I may) proclaim his Gospel worthily and well.

> *At High Mass:*
> In the name of the Father, and of the Son, ✠ and of the Holy Ghost. Amen.

*P/D:* The Lord be with you.
*M:* And with thy spirit.
*P/D:* The beginning (*or* continuation) of the holy Gospel according to N...
*M:* Glory to thee, O Lord.

*M:* Praise to thee, O Christ.

**Stand for the Gospel.**

*S:* Per evangélica dicta deleántur nostra delícta.

# Sermon, when preached

*S:* Credo in unum Deum.

*S/Chorus:* Patrem omnipoténtem, factórem cæli et terræ, visibílium ómnium et invisibílium.

Et in unum Dóminum Iesum Christum, Fílium Dei unigénitum. Et ex Patre natum ante ómnia sǽcula. Deum de Deo, lumen de lúmine, Deum verum de Deo vero. Génitum, non factum, consubstantiálem Patri: per quem ómnia facta sunt. Qui propter nos hómines et propter nostram salútem descéndit de cælis. **Et incarnatus est de Spiritu Sancto ex Maria Virgine: Et homo factus est.** Crucifíxus étiam pro nobis: sub Póntio Piláto passus, et sepúltus est. Et resurréxit tértia die, secúndum Scriptúras. Et ascéndit in cælum, sedet ad déxteram Patris. Et íterum ventúrus est cum glória iudicáre vivos et mórtuos: cuius regni non erit finis.

Et in Spíritum Sanctum, Dóminum et vivificántem: qui ex Patre Filióque procédit. Qui cum Patre et Fílio simul adorátur et conglorificátur: qui locútus est per Prophétas.

Et unam, sanctam, cathólicam et apostólicam Ecclésiam. Confíteor unum baptísma in remissiónem peccatórum. Et exspécto resurrectiónem mortuórum.

Et vitam ✠ ventúri sǽculi. Amen.

*S:* Dóminus vobíscum.
*M:* Et cum spíritu tuo.
*S:* Orémus.

Sermon & Creed

*P:* Through the words of the Gospel may our sins be wiped away.

**Sit for the sermon.**

*The celebrant takes his maniple off to preach.*

*P:* I believe in one God.

*P/Choir:* the Father almighty, maker of heaven and earth, of all things visible and invisible.

And in one Lord Jesus Christ, the Son of God, only begotten, and born of the Father before all ages.

God from God, light from light, true God from true God, begotten, not made, consubstantial with the Father; through him all things were made. For us men and for our salvation he came down from heaven, **and was incarnate by the Holy Ghost from the Virgin Mary, and was made man.** He was crucified also for us under Pontius Pilate, he suffered and was buried, and rose again on the third day in accordance with the Scriptures. And ascended into heaven, and is seated at the right hand of the Father. And he will come again with glory to judge the living and the dead: and his kingdom will have no end.

And in the Holy Ghost, the Lord, the giver of life, who proceeds from the Father and the Son, who together with the Father and the Son is adored and glorified, who has spoken through the Prophets.

And one, holy, catholic and apostolic Church. I confess one baptism for the forgiveness of sins. And I look forward to the resurrection of the dead. And the life ✠ of the world to come. Amen.

**Stand for the Creed; sit when the Priest sits.**

**Genuflect for the embold-ened words.**

*This is the Nicene Creed; the Apostles' Creed is used at Baptisms and the Athanasian Creed at the Rite of Reception.*

*P:* The Lord be with you.

*M:* And with thy spirit.

*P:* Let us pray.

# MISSA FIDELIUM
## Offertorium

### Offertory: see Propers

*S:* Súscipe, sancte Pater, omnípotens ætérne Deus, hanc immaculátam hóstiam, quam ego indígnus fámulus tuus óffero tibi Deo meo vivo et vero, pro innumerabílibus peccátis, et offensiónibus, et neglegéntiis meis, et pro ómnibus circumstántibus, sed et pro ómnibus fidélibus christiánis vivis atque defúnctis: ut mihi, et illis profíciat ad salútem in vitam ætérnam. Amen.

Deus, qui humánæ substántiæ dignitátem mirabíliter condidísti, et mirabílius reformásti: da nobis per huius aquæ et vini mystérium, eius divinitátis esse consórtes, qui humanitátis nostræ fíeri dignátus est párticeps, Iesus Christus, Fílius tuus, Dóminus noster: Qui tecum vivit et regnat in unitáte Spíritus Sancti, Deus, per ómnia sǽcula sæculórum. Amen.

*The offering of the Chalice*

Offérimus tibi, Dómine, cálicem salutáris, tuam deprecántes cleméntiam: ut in conspéctu divínæ maiestátis tuæ, pro nostra et totíus mundi salúte cum odóre suavitátis ascéndat. Amen.

In spíritu humilitátis et in ánimo contríto suscipiámur a te, Dómine: et sic fiat sacrifícium nostrum in conspéctu tuo hódie, ut pláceat tibi, Dómine Deus.

Veni, sanctificátor omnípotens, ætérne Deus: et bénedic ✠ hoc sacrifícium tuo sancto nómini præparátum.

# MASS OF THE FAITHFUL

## Offertory

**Sit for the
Offertory.**

*P:* Receive, O holy Father, almighty and everlasting God, this spotless Victim, which I, thy unworthy servant, offer unto thee, my living and true God, for my numberless sins, offences, and negligences; and for all here present; as also for all faithful Christians living and dead, that it may avail for their salvation and mine, unto life everlasting. Amen.

O God, who wondrously didst create the dignity of human nature and still more wondrously hast restored it: grant that, by the mystery of this water and wine, we may come to share in the divinity of him who humbled himself to share in our humanity, Jesus Christ thy Son, our Lord: who lives and reigns with thee in the unity of the Holy Ghost, one God, for ever and ever. Amen.

We offer unto thee, O Lord, the chalice of salvation, entreating  thy clemency, that it may ascend in the sight of thy divine majesty with an odour of sweetness, for our salvation and for that of the whole world. Amen.

With humble spirit and contrite heart may we be accepted by thee, O Lord, and may our sacrifice in thy sight this day be pleasing to thee, Lord God.

Come, O Sanctifier, almighty and eternal God, and bless ✠ this sacrifice made ready for thy holy name.

*At Sung and High Mass incense is blessed, and the Offerings, and then the Faithful, are incensed.*

Per intercessiónem beáti Michaélis Archángeli, stantis a dextris altáris incénsi, et ómnium electórum suórum, incénsum istud dignétur Dóminus benedícere ✠ et in odórem suavitátis accípere. Per Christum Dóminum nostrum. Amen.

Incensum istud a te benedíctum, ascéndat ad te, Dómine: et descéndat super nos misericórdia tua.

Dirigatur, Dómine, orátio mea, sicut incénsum in conspéctu tuo: elevátio mánuum meárum sacrifícium vespertínum. Pone, Dómine, custódiam ori meo, et óstium circumstántiæ lábiis meis: Ut non declínet cor meum in verba malítiæ, ad excusándas excusatiónes in peccátis.

Accendat in nobis Dóminus ignem sui amóris, et flammam ætérnæ caritátis. Amen.

*S:* Lavábo inter innocéntes manus meas: et circúmdabo altáre tuum, Dómine: Ut áudiam vocem laudis, et enárrem univérsa mirabília tua. Dómine, diléxi decórem domus tuæ, et locum habitatiónis glóriæ tuæ. Ne perdas cum ímpiis, Deus, ánimam meam, et cum viris sánguinum vitam meam: In quorum mánibus iniquitátes sunt: déxtera eórum repléta est munéribus. Ego autem in innocéntia mea ingréssus sum: rédime me, et miserére mei. Pes meus stetit in dirécto: in ecclésiis benedícam te, Dómine. Glória Patri.

*S:* Súscipe, sancta Trínitas, hanc oblatiónem, quam tibi offérimus ob memóriam passiónis, resurrectiónis et ascensiónis Iesu Christi, Dómini nostri: et in honórem beátæ Maríæ semper Vírginis, et beáti Ioánnis Baptístæ, et sanctórum Apostolórum Petri et Pauli, et istórum, et ómnium Sanctórum: ut illis profíciat ad honórem, nobis autem ad salútem: et illi pro nobis intercédere dignéntur in cælis, quorum memóriam ágimus in terris. Per eúndem Christum Dóminum nostrum. Amen.

*S:* Orate, fratres: ut meum ac vestrum sacrifícium acceptábile fiat apud Deum Patrem omnipoténtem.

Through the intercession of blessed Michael the Archangel standing at the right hand of the altar of incense, and of all his elect, may the Lord be pleased to bless ✠ this incense, and to receive it in the odour of sweetness. Through Christ Our Lord. Amen.

May this incense which thou hast blessed, O Lord, ascend to thee, and may thy mercy descend upon us.

Let my prayer, O Lord, be directed as incense in thy sight; the lifting up of my hands as an evening sacrifice. Set a watch, O Lord, before my mouth, and a door round about my lips: That my heart may not incline to evil words, and seek excuses in sins.

May the Lord kindle within us the fire of his love, and the flame of everlasting charity. Amen.

**Stand and bow to be incensed, then sit.**

*P:* I will wash my hands among the innocent: and will compass thy altar, O Lord. That I may hear the voice of thy praise, and tell of all thy wondrous works. I have loved, O Lord, the beauty of thy house, and the place where thy glory dwells. Take not away my soul, O God, with the wicked, nor my life with bloody men: in whose hands are iniquities: their right hand is filled with gifts. But as for me, I have walked in my innocence: redeem me, and have mercy on me. My foot has stood in the direct way: in the churches I will bless thee, O Lord. Glory be to the Father.

*The Priest washes his hands while saying the Psalm* Lavabo *in a low voice.*

*P:* Receive, O Holy Trinity, this oblation which we offer unto thee in memory of the passion, resurrection and ascension of our Lord Jesus Christ, and in honour of blessed Mary ever-Virgin, of blessed John the Baptist, of the holy Apostles Peter and Paul, of these, and of all the saints: that it may avail them for honour and us for salvation: and that they may be pleased to intercede for us in heaven whose commemoration we make on earth. Through the same Christ our Lord. Amen.

*The Priest returns to the centre of the Altar, and prays silently.*

*P:* Pray, brethren, that my sacrifice and yours may be acceptable to God the almighty Father.

*M:* Suscípiat Dóminus sacrifícium de mánibus tuis, ad laude et glóriam nóminis sui, ad utilitátem quoque nostram, totiúsque Ecclésiæ suæ sanctæ.

*S:* Amen.

*The Priest says the final words of the Secret Prayer aloud.*

## Secret: see Propers

*S:* **...per ómnia sǽcula sæculórum.**

*M:* Amen.

*S:* Dóminus vobíscum.

*M:* Et cum spíritu tuo.

*S:* Sursum corda.

*M:* Habémus ad Dóminum.

*S:* Grátias agámus Dómino Deo nostro.

*M:* Dignum et iustum est.

## Præfatio

*The Preface for Trinity printed here is used for most Sundays; for other Prefaces, see pp40–1.*

*S:* Vere dignum et iustum est, æquum et salutáre, nos tibi semper, et ubíque grátias ágere: Dómine, sancte Pater, omnípotens ætérne Deus: Qui cum unigénito Fílio tuo et Spíritu Sancto, unus es Deus, unus es Dóminus: non in uníus singularitáte persónæ, sed in uníus Trinitáte substántiæ. Quod enim de tua glória, revelánte te, crédimus, hoc de Fílio tuo, hoc de Spíritu Sancto, sine differéntia discretiónis sentímus. Ut in confessióne veræ sempiternǽque Deitátis, et in persónis propríetas, et in esséntia únitas, et in maiestáte adorétur æquálitas. Quam laudant Angeli atque Archángeli, Chérubim quoque ac Séraphim: qui non cessant clamáre cotídie, una voce dicéntes:

*The Sanctus is Sung by the Choir and Faithful in Sung Masses. Two Chant settings of Sanctus are found on pp61 & 63.*

Sanctus, Sanctus, Sanctus, Dóminus, Deus Sábaoth.
Pleni sunt cæli et terra glória tua. Hosánna in excélsis.
Benedíctus, qui venit in nómine Dómini. Hosánna in excélsis.

*M:* May the Lord accept the sacrifice at thy hands, for the praise and glory of his name, for our good and the good of all his holy Church.

*P:* Amen.


*P:* **...for ever and ever.**
*M:* Amen.
*P:* The Lord be with you.
*M:* And with thy spirit.
*P:* Lift up your hearts.
*M:* We lift them up to the Lord.
*P:* Let us give thanks to the Lord our God.
*M:* It is right and just.

# Preface

*P:* It is truly right and just, our duty and our salvation, always and everywhere to give thee thanks, Lord, holy Father, almighty and eternal God. For with thy only begotten Son and the Holy Ghost thou art one God, one Lord: not in the unity of a single person, but in a Trinity of one substance. For what thou hast revealed to us of thy glory, we believe equally of thy Son and of the Holy Ghost without difference or distinction, so that, in the confessing of the true and eternal Godhead, thou mayest be adored in what is proper to each Person, their unity in substance, and their equality in majesty. For this is praised by Angels and Archangels, Cherubim too, and Seraphim, who never cease to cry out each day, as with one voice they acclaim:

**At Sung Masses, stand.**

Holy, Holy, Holy, Lord God of hosts. Heaven and earth are full of thy glory. Hosanna in the highest. Blessed is he who comes in the name of the Lord. Hosanna in the highest.

**At the Sanctus, kneel. At Low Mass, remain kneeling until the Last Gospel.**

# Canon Missæ

*Prayer for the Church*

Te ígitur, clementíssime Pater, per Iesum Christum, Fílium tuum, Dóminum nostrum, súpplices rogámus, ac pétimus, uti accépta hábeas et benedícas, hæc ✠ dona, hæc ✠ múnera, hæc ✠ sancta sacrifica illibáta, in primis, quæ tibi offérimus pro Ecclésia tua sancta cathólica: quam pacificáre, custodíre, adunáre, et régere dignéris toto orbe terrárum: una cum fámulo tuo Papa nostro N., et Antístite nostro N., et ómnibus orthodóxis atque cathólicæ et apostólicæ fídei cultóribus.

*Prayer for the Living*

Memento, Dómine, famulórum famularúmque tuárum N. et N. et ómnium circumstántium, quorum tibi fides cogníta est, et nota devótio, pro quibus tibi offérimus: vel qui tibi ófferunt hoc sacrifícium laudis, pro se suísque ómnibus: pro redemptióne animárum suárum, pro spe salútis et incolumitátis suæ: tibíque reddunt vota sua ætérno Deo, vivo et vero.

*Invocation of the Saints*

Communicaántes, et memóriam venerántes, in primis gloriósæ semper Vírginis Maríæ, Genetrícis Dei et Dómini nostri Iesu Christi: sed et beati Ioseph eiusdem Vírginis Sponsi, et beatórum Apostolórum ac Mártyrum tuórum, Petri et Pauli, Andréæ, Iacóbi, Ioánnis, Thomæ, Iacóbi, Philíppi, Bartholomǽi, Matthǽi, Simónis et Thaddǽi, Lini, Cleti, Cleméntis, Xysti, Cornélii, Cypriáni, Lauréntii, Chrysógoni, Ioánnis et Pauli, Cosmæ et Damiáni, et ómnium Sanctórum tuórum; quorum méritis precibúsque concédas, ut in ómnibus protectiónis tuæ muniámur auxílio. Per eúndem Christum Dóminum nostrum. Amen.

# The Canon of the Mass

To thee, therefore, most merciful Father, we make humble prayer and petition through Jesus Christ, thy Son, our Lord: that thou accept and bless these ✠ gifts, these ✠ offerings, these ✠ holy and unblemished sacrifices, which we offer thee first of all for thy holy catholic Church. Be pleased to grant her peace, to guard, unite and govern her throughout the whole world, together with thy servant N. our Pope and N. our Bishop, and all those who, holding to the truth, hand on the catholic and apostolic faith.

*The Canon is said silently.*

Remember, Lord, thy servants and handmaids N. and N. and all gathered here, whose faith and devotion are known to thee. For them we offer thee this sacrifice of praise, or they offer it for themselves and all who are dear to them, for the redemption of their souls, in hope of health and well-being, and fulfilling their vows to thee, the eternal God, living and true.

*The Priest calls to mind the living for whom he wants to pray.*

In communion with those whose memory we venerate, especially the glorious ever-Virgin Mary, Mother of our God and Lord Jesus Christ, and blessed Joseph, Spouse of the same Virgin, and thy blessed Apostles and Martyrs Peter and Paul, Andrew, James, John, Thomas, James, Philip, Bartholomew, Matthew, Simon and Thaddeus, Linus, Cletus, Clement, Xystus, Cornelius, Cyprian, Lawrence, Chrysogonus, John and Paul, Cosmas and Damian and all thy Saints; through their merits and prayers grant that in all things we may be defended by thy protecting help. Through the same Christ our Lord. Amen.

*St Joseph was added to the list of saints in 1962.*

*Oblation of
the Victim*

Hanc ígitur oblatiónem servitútis nostræ, sed et cunctæ famíliæ tuæ, quǽsumus, Dómine, ut placátus accípias: diésque nostros in tua pace dispónas, atque ab ætérna damnatióne nos éripi, et in electórum tuórum iúbeas grege numerári. Per Christum Dóminum nostrum. Amen.

Quam oblatiónem tu, Deus, in ómnibus, quǽsumus, benedíctam ✠, adscríptam ✠, ratam ✠, rationábilem, acceptabilémque fácere dignéris: ut nobis Corpus ✠,et Sanguis ✠ fiat dilectíssimi Fílii tui Dómini nostri Iesu Christi.

Qui prídie quam paterétur, accépit panem in sanctas ac venerábiles manus suas, et elevátis óculis in cælum ad te Deum, Patrem suum omnipoténtem, tibi grátias agens, benedíxit ✠, fregit, dedítque discípulis suis, dicens: Accípite, et manducáte ex hoc omnes.

*Consecrations*
🔔🔔🔔

### HOC EST ENIM CORPUS MEUM.

*The bell is
rung three
times for each
Consecration,
of the Host
and the Chal-
ice.*

Símili modo postquam cenátum est, accípiens et hunc præclárum Cálicem in sanctas ac venerábiles manus suas: item tibi grátias agens, benedíxit ✠, dedítque discípulis suis, dicens: Accípite, et bíbite ex eo omnes.

### HIC EST ENIM CALIX SANGUINIS MEI, NOVI ET ÆTERNI TESTAMENTI: MYSTERIUM FIDEI: QUI PRO VOBIS ET PRO MULTIS EFFUNDETUR IN REMISSIONEM PECCATORUM.

🔔🔔🔔

*Offering of the
Victim*

Hæc quotiescúmque fecéritis, in mei memóriam faciétis.

Therefore, Lord, we pray: graciously accept this oblation of our service, that of your whole family: order our
days in thy peace, and command that we be delivered
from eternal damnation and counted among the flock
of those thou hast chosen. Through Christ our Lord.
Amen.

*The bell is rung.*

Be pleased, O God, we pray, to bless ✠, acknowledge
✠ , and approve ✠ this offering in every respect; make
it spiritual and acceptable, so that it may become for us
the Body ✠ and Blood ✠ of thy most beloved Son, our
Lord Jesus Christ.

On the day before he was to suffer, he took bread in his
holy and venerable hands, and with eyes raised to
heaven to thee, O God, his almighty Father, giving
thanks to thee, he blessed,✠ broke the bread and gave
it to his disciples, saying: Take this, all of you, and eat
of it,

FOR THIS IS MY BODY.

Likewise, when supper was ended, he took this precious chalice in his holy and venerable hands, and once
more giving thanks to thee, he blessed,✠ and gave the
chalice to his disciples, saying: Take this, all of you,
and drink from it,

FOR THIS IS THE CHALICE OF MY  BLOOD,
THE BLOOD OF THE NEW AND  ETERNAL COV-
ENANT: THE MYSTERY OF FAITH: WHICH
WILL BE POURED OUT FOR YOU AND FOR
MANY FOR THE FORGIVENESS OF SINS.

As often as ye shall do these things, ye shall do them in
memory of me.

Unde et mémores, Dómine, nos servi tui, sed et plebs tua sancta, eiúsdem Christi Fílii tui, Dómini nostri, tam beátæ passiónis, nec non et ab ínferis resurrectiónis, sed et in cælos gloriósæ ascensiónis : offérimus præcláræ maiestáti tuæ, de tuis donis ac datis, hóstiam ✠ puram, hóstiam ✠ sanctam, hóstiam ✠ immaculátam, Panem ✠ sanctum vitæ ætérnæ, et Cálicem ✠ salútis perpétuæ.

*Prayer for Blessings*

Supra quæ propítio ac seréno vultu respícere dignéris: et accépta habére, sicúti accépta habére dignátus es múnera púeri tui iusti Abel, et sacrifícium patriárchæ nostri Abrahæ: et quod tibi óbtulit summus sacérdos tuus Melchísedech, sanctum sacrifícium, immaculátam hóstiam.

*Prayer for the Dead*

Súpplices te rogámus, omnípotens Deus: iube hæc perférri per manus sancti Angeli tui in sublíme altáre tuum, in conspéctu divínæ maiestátis tuæ: ut quotquot ex hac altáris participatióne sacrosánctum Fílii tui Corpus ✠ et Sánguinem ✠ sumpsérimus, omni benedictióne cælésti et grátia repleámur. Per eúndem Christum Dóminum nostrum. Amen.

Meménto étiam, Dómine, famulórum, famularúmque tuárum N. et N. qui nos præcessérunt cum signo fídei, et dórmiunt in somno pacis.

Ipsis, Dómine, et ómnibus in Christo quiescéntibus locum refrigérii, lucis et pacis, ut indúlgeas, deprecámur. Per eúndem Christum Dóminum nostrum. Amen.

*The Priest says the words 'Nobis quoque peccatoribus' aloud, recalling his own sinfulness.*

**Nobis quoque peccatóribus** fámulis tuis, de multitúdine miseratiónum tuárum sperántibus, partem áliquam, et societátem donáre dignéris, cum tuis sanctis Apóstolis et Martyribus: cum Ioánne, Stéphano, Matthía, Bárnaba, Ignátio, Alexándro, Marcellíno, Petro,

Therefore, O Lord, as we celebrate the memorial of the blessed Passion, of the Resurrection from the dead, and the glorious Ascension into heaven of Christ, thy Son, our Lord, we thy servants and thy holy people, offer to thy glorious majesty from the gifts that thou hast given us, this pure ✠ victim, this holy ✠ victim, this spotless ✠ victim, the holy ✠ Bread of eternal life, and the Chalice ✠ of everlasting salvation.

Be pleased to look upon them with serene and kindly countenance, and accept them, as once thou wast pleased to accept the gifts of thy servant Abel, the just, the sacrifice of Abraham our father in faith, and the offering of thy high priest Melchizedek, a holy sacrifice, a spotless victim.

In humble prayer we ask thee, almighty God: command that these gifts be borne by the hands of thy holy Angel to thine altar on high in the sight of thy divine majesty, that all of us who through this participation at the altar receive the most holy Body ✠ and Blood ✠ of thy Son may be filled with every grace and heavenly blessing. Through the same Christ our Lord. Amen.

Remember also, Lord, thy servants and handmaids N. and N. who have gone before us with the sign of faith and rest in the sleep of peace.

*The Priest mentions the dead for whom he wishes to pray.*

Grant them, O Lord, we pray, and all who sleep in Christ, a place of refreshment, light and peace. Through the same Christ our Lord. Amen.

**To us, also, thy sinful servants** who hope in thy abundant mercies, graciously grant some share and fellowship with thy holy Apostles and Martyrs: with John, Stephen, Matthias, Barnabas, Ignatius, Alexander, Marcellinus, Peter, Felicity, Perpetua, Agatha, Lucy,

*The Priest strikes his breast.*

Felicitáte, Perpétua, Agatha, Lúcia, Agnéte, Cæcília, Anastásia, et ómnibus Sanctis tuis: intra quorum nos consórtium, non æstimátor mériti, sed véniæ, quæsumus, largítor admítte. Per Christum Dóminum nostrum.

Per quem hæc ómnia, Dómine, semper bona creas, sanctíficas ✠, vivíficas ✠, benedícis ✠, et præstas nobis.

*Final Doxology The Priest raises his voice to conclude the Canon.*

Per ipsum ✠, et cum ipso ✠, et in ipso ✠ est tibi Deo Patri ✠ omnipoténti in unitáte Spíritus ✠ Sancti omnis honor, et glória, **per ómnia sǽcula sæculórum.**
*M:* Amen.

# Communio

*The Priest continues aloud.*

*The Pater Noster*

*S:* Orémus.
Præcéptis salutáribus móniti, et divína institutióne formáti, audémus dícere:
Pater noster, qui es in cælis: Sanctificétur nomen tuum: Advéniat regnum tuum: Fiat volúntas tua, sicut in cælo, et in terra. Panem nostrum cotidiánum da nobis hódie: Et dimítte nobis débita nostra, sicut et nos dimíttimus debitóribus nostris. Et ne nos indúcas in tentatiónem.
*M:* Sed líbera nos a malo.
*S:* Amen.
Líbera nos, quǽsumus, Dómine, ab ómnibus malis, prætéritis, præséntibus et futúris: et intercedénte beáta et gloriósa semper Vírgine Dei Genetríce María, cum beátis Apóstolis tuis Petro et Paulo, atque Andréa, et ómnibus Sanctis, da propítius pacem in diébus nostris: ut, ope misericórdiæ tuæ adiúti, et a peccáto simus semper líberi, et ab omni perturbatióne secúri. Per eún-

Agnes, Cecilia, Anastasia and all thy Saints: admit us, we beseech thee, into their company, not weighing our merits, but granting us thy pardon, through Christ our Lord.

Through whom thou dost continue to create all these good things, O Lord; thou dost make them ✠ holy, fill them ✠ with life, bless ✠ them, and bestow them upon us.

*At the 'Per ipsum' the Priest uncovers the Chalice, genuflects, and makes the sign of the cross over the Chalice with the Host, five times.*

Through ✠ him, and with ✠ him, and in ✠ him, to thee, O God, almighty ✠ Father, in the unity of the Ho-ly ✠ Ghost, is all honour and glory, **for ever and ever.** *M:* Amen.

# Communion Rites

*P:* Let us pray.
At the Saviour's command and formed by divine teaching, we dare to say:
Our Father who art in heaven, hallowed be thy name; thy kingdom come, thy will be done on earth as it is in heaven. Give us this day our daily bread, and forgive us our trespasses, as we forgive those who trespass against us; and lead us not into temptation.

**At Sung Masses, stand for the *Pater Noster.***

*R:* But deliver us from evil.
*P:* Amen.
Deliver us, Lord, we pray, from every evil, past, pre-sent and to come, and by the intercession of the blessed and glorious ever-Virgin Mary, Mother of God, with thy blessed Apostles Peter and Paul, and Andrew, and all the Saints, graciously grant peace in our days, that, by the help of thy mercy, we may be always free from sin and safe from all distress. Through the same Jesus

dem Dóminum nostrum Iesum Christum Fílium tuum, qui tecum vivit et regnat in unitáte Spíritus Sancti Deus, per ómnia sǽcula sæculórum.

*M:* Amen.

*S:* Pax ✠ Dómini sit ✠ semper ✠ vobíscum.

*M:* Et cum spíritu tuo.

*Prayers of Preparation for Holy Communion*

Hæc commíxtio, et consecrátio Córporis et Sánguinis Dómini nostri Iesu Christi, fiat accipiéntibus nobis in vitam ætérnam. Amen.

Agnus Dei, qui tollis peccáta mundi: miserére nobis.

Agnus Dei, qui tollis peccáta mundi: miserére nobis.
Agnus Dei, qui tollis peccáta mundi: dona nobis pacem.

Domine Iesu Christe, qui dixísti Apóstolis tuis: Pacem relínquo vobis, pacem meam do vobis: ne respícias peccáta mea, sed fidem Ecclésiæ tuæ; eámque secúndum voluntátem tuam pacificáre et coadunáre dignéris: Qui vivis et regnas Deus per ómnia sǽcula sæculórum. Amen.

> *S:* Pax tecum.
> *D:* Et cum spíritu tuo.

Dómine Iesu Christe, Fili Dei vivi, qui ex voluntáte Patris, cooperánte Spíritu sancto, per mortem tuam mundum vivificásti: líbera me per hoc sacrosánctum Corpus et Sánguinem tuum ab ómnibus iniquitátibus meis, et univérsis malis: et fac me tuis semper inhærére mandátis, et a te numquam separári permíttas: Qui cum eódem Deo Patre et Spíritu Sancto vivis et regnas Deus in sǽcula sæculórum. Amen.

Christ thy Son our Lord, who lives and reigns with thee in the unity of the Holy Ghost, one God, for ever and ever.

*M:* Amen

*P:* The peace ✠ of the Lord be ✠ with you ✠ always.

*M:* And with thy spirit.

*The Priest makes the sign of the Cross with a particle of the Host, three times over the Chalice before dropping it into the Chalice.*

May this mingling and consecration of the Body and Blood of our Lord Jesus Christ bring eternal life to us who receive it. Amen.

Lamb of God, who takest away the sins of the world, have mercy on us.

Lamb of God, who takest away the sins of the world, have mercy on us.

Lamb of God, who takest away the sins of the world, grant us peace.

Lord Jesus Christ, who said to thy Apostles, Peace I leave you, my peace I give you; look not on my sins but on the faith of thy Church; and graciously grant her peace and unity in accordance with thy will. Who livest and reignest God, for ever and ever. Amen.

*In High and Pontifical Mass the Sacred Ministers exchange the Kiss of Peace during the singing of the Agnus Dei.*

*P:* Peace be with thee.

*D:* And with thy spirit.

Lord Jesus Christ, Son of the living God, who by the will of the Father and the work of the Holy Ghost, through thy death gavest life to the world, free me by this thy most holy Body and Blood from all my sins and from every evil; keep me always faithful to thy commandments, and never let me be parted from thee; who with the same God the Father and the Holy Ghost livest and reignest God, for ever and ever. Amen.

May the receiving of thy Body and Blood, Lord Jesus Christ, which I though unworthy presume to take, not

Percéptio Corpóris tui, Dómine Iesu Christe, quod ego indígnus súmere præsumo, non mihi provéniat in iudícium et condemnatiónem: sed pro tua pietáte prosit mihi ad tutaméntum mentis et córporis, et ad medélam percipiéndam: Qui vivis et regnas cum Deo Patre in unitáte Spíritus Sancti Deus, per ómnia sǽcula sæculórum. Amen.

*The Priest receives the Host.*

Panem cæléstem accípiam, et nomen Dómini invocábo.

Dómine, non sum dignus, ut intres sub tectum meum: sed tantum dic verbo et sanábitur ánima mea. (*ter*)

Corpus Dómini nostri Iesu Christi custódiat ánimam meam in vitam ætérnam. Amen.

*The Priest receives the Chalice.*

Quid retríbuam Dómino pro ómnibus quæ retríbuit mihi? Cálicem salutáris accípiam, et nomen Dómini invocábo. Laudans invocábo Dóminum, et ab inimícis meis salvus ero.

*The Priest shows the Host to the Faithful.*

Sanguis Dómini nostri Iesu Christi custódiat ánimam meam in vitam ætérnam. Amen.

Ecce Agnus Dei: ecce qui tollit peccáta mundi.

Dómine, non sum dignus ut intres sub tectum meum; sed tantum dic verbo et sanábitur ánima mea. (*ter*)

*The Host is given to each communicant with these words.*

Corpus Dómini nostri Iesu Christi custódiat ánimam tuam in vitam ætérnam. Amen.

bring me to judgment and condemnation, but through thy loving mercy may it be for me protection in mind and body; who livest and reignest with God the Father in the unity of the Holy Ghost, God, for ever and ever. Amen.

I will take the bread of heaven, and call upon the name of the Lord.

Lord, I am not worthy that thou shouldst enter under my roof; but only say the word and my soul shall be healed. *(three times)*

May the body of our Lord Jesus Christ keep my soul safe unto eternal life. Amen.

What shall I render to the Lord for all the things he hath rendered to me? I will take the chalice of salvation, and will call upon the name of the Lord. With praise I will call upon the Lord, and I shall be saved from my enemies.

May the Blood of our Lord Jesus Christ keep my soul safe unto eternal life. Amen.

Behold the Lamb of God, behold him who takes away the sins of the world.

Lord, I am not worthy that thou shouldst enter under my roof, but only say the word and my soul shall be healed. *(three times)*

May the Body of our Lord Jesus Christ keep thy soul safe unto eternal life. Amen .

♤♤♤
*The bell is rung three times.*

**At the Vetus Ordo, Holy Communion is received kneeling (if possible) and on the tongue.**

*In some places the Confiteor is said at this point, as on p6.*

31

# Postcommunio

Quod ore súmpsimus, Dómine, pura mente capiámus: et de múnere temporáli fiat nobis remédium sempitérnum.

Corpus tuum, Dómine, quod sumpsi, et Sanguis, quem potávi, adhǽreat viscéribus meis: et præsta, ut in me non remáneat scélerum mácula, quem pura et sancta refecérunt sacraménta: Qui vivis et regnas in sǽcula sæculórum. Amen.

## Communion antiphon: see Propers

*S:* Dóminus vobíscum.
*M:* Et cum spíritu tuo.
*S:* Oremus.

## Postcommunion prayer: see Propers

*M:* Amen.
*S:* Dóminus vobíscum.
*M:* Et cum spíritu tuo.
*S/D:* Ite, missa est. [*vel:* Benedicamus Domino.]
*M:* Deo grátias.

Pláceat tibi, sancta Trínitas, obséquium servitútis meæ: et præsta: ut sacrifícium, quod óculis tuæ maiestátis indígnus óbtuli, tibi sit acceptábile, mihíque et ómnibus, pro quibus illud óbtuli, sit, te miseránte, propitiábile. Per Christum Dóminum nostrum. Amen.

*When the celebrant is a Bishop, his blessing is introduced with this dialogue.*

*Episcopus:* Sit nomen Dómini benedíctum.
*Omnes:* Ex hoc nunc et usque in sæculum.
*E:* Adiutórium nostrum in nómine Dómini.
*O:* Qui fecit cælum et terram.

# Prayers after Communion

What has passed our lips as food, O Lord, may we possess in purity of heart, that what has been given to us in time may be our healing for eternity.

   May thy Body, Lord, which I have received, and thy Blood which I have drunk, cleave to my inmost parts, and grant that no stain of sin may remain in me, whom these pure and holy sacraments have refreshed. Who livest and reignest for ever and ever. Amen.

*The Chalice is cleansed by the pouring of wine and water over the fingers of the Priest into it, which is consumed by the Priest.*

*P:* The Lord be with you.
*M:* And with thy spirit.
*P:* Let us pray.

*M:* Amen.
*P:* The Lord be with you.
*M:* And with thy spirit.
*P.* Go, you are dismissed. [*Or:* Let us bless the Lord.]
*M:* Thanks be to God.

May the tribute of my homage be pleasing to thee, most holy Trinity; and grant that the sacrifice which I, unworthy as I am, have offered in the sight of thy majesty may be acceptable to thee; and through thy mercy may it bring forgiveness to me and all for whom I have offered it. Through Christ our Lord. Amen.

**Kneel for the blessing.**

> *Bishop:* Blessed be the name of the Lord.
> *All:* From henceforth, now and forever.
> *B.:* Our help is in the name of the Lord.
> *All:* Who made heaven and earth.

Benedicat vos omnípotens Deus, Pater, et Filíus ✠, et Spíritus Sanctus.
*M:* Amen.

## Ultimum Evangelium

*S:* Dóminus vobíscum.
*M:* Et cum spíritu tuo.
*S:* ✠ Inítium sancti Evangélii secúndum Ioánnem.

*M:* Glória tibi, Dómine.

*S:* In princípio erat Verbum, et Verbum erat apud Deum, et Deus erat Verbum. Hoc erat in princípio apud Deum. Omnia per ipsum facta sunt: et sine ipso factum est nihil, quod factum est: in ipso vita erat, et vita erat lux hóminum: et lux in ténebris lucet, et ténebræ eam non comprehendérunt.

Fuit homo missus a Deo, cui nomen erat Ioánnes. Hic venit in testimónium, ut testimónium perhibéret de lúmine, ut omnes créderent per illum. Non erat ille lux, sed ut testimónium perhibéret de lúmine. Erat lux vera, quæ illúminat omnem hóminem veniéntem in hunc mundum. In mundo erat, et mundus per ipsum factus est, et mundus eum non cognóvit. In própria venit, et sui eum non recepérunt. Quotquot autem recepérunt eum, dedit eis potestátem fílios Dei fíeri, his, qui credunt in nómine eius: qui non ex sanguínibus, neque ex voluntáte carnis, neque ex voluntáte viri, sed ex Deo nati sunt. **ET VERBUM CARO FACTUM EST**, et habitávit in nobis: et vídimus glóriam eius, glóriam quasi Unigéniti a Patre, plenum grátiæ et veritátis.
*M:* Deo grátias.

*Prayers of thanksgiving after Communion are found on pp45–7.*

May almighty God bless you, the Father, the Son ✠, and the Holy Ghost.

*M:* Amen.

# The Last Gospel

*P:* The Lord be with you.

*M:* And with thy spirit.

*P:* ✠ The beginning of the holy Gospel according to John.

*M:* Glory to thee, O Lord.

*P:* In the beginning was the Word, and the Word was with God, and the Word was God. The same was in the beginning with God. All things were made by him, and without him was made nothing that was made. In him was life, and the life was the light of men: and the light shineth in darkness, and the darkness did not comprehend it.

There was a man sent from God, whose name was John. This man came for a witness, to bear witness of the light, that all men through him might believe. He was not the light, but was to bear witness of the light. That was the true light, which enlighteneth every man, that cometh into this world. He was in the world, and the world was made by him, and the world knew him not. He came unto his own, and his own received him not. But as many as received him, to them gave he power to be made the sons of God: to them that believe in his name: who were born, not of blood, nor of the will of the flesh, nor of the will of man, but of God. **AND THE WORD WAS MADE FLESH**, and dwelt among us: and we saw his glory, the glory as of the Only Begotten of the Father, full of grace and truth.

*M:* Thanks be to God.

Kneel at the emboldened words.

*Turn the page for the Prayer for the Sovereign on Sundays, and two pages for Prayers after Low Mass.*

# Oratio pro Regina

*Sung or said after the Principal Mass on Sunday, in England and Wales.*

*At the principal Mass on Sunday, Prayers for the Sovereign follow in England and Wales; at Low Mass, Prayers After Low Mass follow. If both are said, the Prayer for the Sovereign is said first.*

*Cantor:* Dómine, salvam fac
*Omnes:* Reginam nostram Elísabeth, Et exáudi nos in die, qua invocavérimus te.

I.

Dómine, salvam fac ✳ regínam nostram E- lísabeth: et ex-
*For the King:* salvum fac ✳ re- gem nostrum

audi nos in di- e, qua invocavé- rimus te.

*S:* Oremus.

Quǽsumus, omnípotens Deus, ut famula tua Elísabeth, Regína nostra, quæ tua miseratióne suscépit regni gubernácula, virtútum étiam ómnium percípiat increménta; quibus decénter ornáta et vitiórum monstra devitáre, (*in time of war:* hostes superáre), et ad te qui via, véritas, et vita es, cum Principe consorte et prole régia gratiósa valeat perv022 veníre. Per Christum Dóminum nostrum.

*R:* Amen.

*In England and Wales, after a Sung Mass a Marian Anthem is often sung: see pp66–8.*

# Prayer for the Sovereign

*Sung or said after the Principal Mass on Sunday, in England and Wales.*

*Cantor:* O Lord, save
*All:* Elizabeth our Queen. And mercifully hear us when
we call upon thee.

*Turn the page for the 'Prayers after Low Mass'.*

*The chant setting for the Domine salvam fac.*

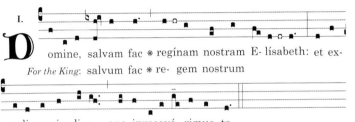

omine, salvam fac * regínam nostram E- lísabeth: et ex-

*For the King:* salvum fac * re- gem nostrum

audi nos in di- e, qua invocavé- rimus te.

*P:* Let us pray.
We beseech thee, almighty God, that thy servant Elizabeth our Queen, who through thy mercy has undertaken the government of this realm, may also receive an increase of all virtues. Fittingly adorned with these, may she be able to shun all evildoing, [*in time of war:* to vanquish her enemies,] and, together with the Prince her consort and the royal family, being in thy grace, to come unto thee who art the way, the truth, and the life. Through Christ our Lord.
*R:* Amen.

# Orationes post Missam

*Also called the 'Leonine Prayers', in 1930 Pius XI ordered them to be said for Russia.*

*They may not be said if other ceremonies follow Mass immediately.*

*S:* Ave Maria, grátia plena, Dóminus tecum; benedícta tu in muliéribus, et benedíctus fructus ventris tui, Iesus.
*R:* Sancta María, Mater Dei, ora pro nobis peccatóribus, nunc et in hora mortis nostræ. Amen. *(ter)*

Salve Regína, Mater misericórdiæ; vita, dulcédo et spes nostra, salve. Ad te clamámus, éxsules fílii Evæ. Ad te suspirámus, geméntes et flentes in hac lacrimarum valle. Eia ergo, advocáta nostra, illos tuos misericórdes óculos ad nos convérte. Et Iesum, benedíctum fructum ventris tui, nobis, post hoc exsílium, osténde. O clemens, o pia, o dulcis Virgo María .

*S:* Ora pro nobis, sancta Dei Génetrix.
*R:* Ut digni efficiámur promissiónibus Christi.

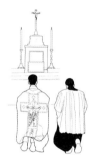

*S:* Orémus
Deus, refúgium nostrum et virtus, pópulum ad te clamántem propítius réspice; et intercedénte gloriósa et immaculáta Virgine Dei Genetríce María, cum beáto Ioseph, eius Sponso, ac beátis Apóstolis tuis Petro et Paulo, et ómnibus Sanctis, quas pro conversióne peccatórum, pro libertáte et exaltatióne sanctæ Matris Ecclésiæ, preces effúndimus, miséricors et benígnus exáudi. Per eúndem Christum Dóminum nostrum.
*R:* Amen.
*S:* Sancte Míchaéle Archángele, defénde nos in proélio, contra nequítiam et insídias diáboli esto præsídium. Ímperet illi Deus, súpplices deprecámur: tuque, princeps milítiæ cæléstis, Sátanam aliósque spíritus malígnos, qui ad perditiónem animárum pervagántur in mundo, divína virtúte in inférnum detrúde.
*R:* Amen.
*S:* Cor Iesu sacratíssimum,
*R:* Miserére nobis. *(ter)*

# Prayers after Low Mass

*P:* Hail, Mary, full of grace, the Lord is with thee; blessed art thou amongst women, and blessed is the fruit of thy womb, Jesus.

*R:* Holy Mary, Mother of God, pray for us sinners, now and at the hour of our death. Amen. *(three times)*

Hail, holy Queen, Mother of mercy; hail, our life, our sweetness and our hope. To thee do we cry, poor banished children of Eve. To thee do we send up our sighs, mourning and weeping in this vale of tears. Turn then, most gracious advocate, thine eyes of mercy towards us. And after this our exile, show unto us the blessed fruit of thy womb, Jesus. O clement, O loving, O sweet Virgin Mary.

*P:* Pray for us, O holy Mother of God.

*R:* That we may be made worthy of the promises of Christ.

*P:* Let us pray.

O God, our refuge and our strength, look down in mercy on thy people who cry to thee; and by the intercession of the glorious and immaculate Virgin Mary, Mother of God, of St Joseph her spouse, of thy blessed Apostles Peter and Paul, and of all the saints, in mercy and goodness hear our prayers for the conversion of sinners, and for the liberty and exaltation of our holy Mother the Church. Through the same Christ our Lord.

*R:* Amen.

*P:* Holy Michael Archangel, defend us in the day of battle; be our safeguard against the wickedness and snares of the devil. May God rebuke him, we humbly pray, and do thou, prince of the heavenly host, by the power of God thrust down to hell Satan and all wicked spirits, who wander through the world for the ruin of souls.

*R:* Amen.

*P:* Most Sacred Heart of Jesus,

*R:* Have mercy on us. *(three times)*

*Prayers After Low Mass were instituted by Pope Pius IX in 1859, and made universal by Pope Leo XIII in 1884.*

*This collect was adapted and the Prayer to St Michael added in 1886.*

*The invocation of the Sacred Heart was added by Pope St Pius X in 1904.*

# Other Prefaces: Common Preface

Vere dignum et iustum est, æquum et salutáre, nos tibi semper, et ubíque grátias ágere: Dómine, sancte Pater, omnípotens, ætérne Deus: per Christum Dóminum nostrum. Per quem maiestátem tuam laudant Angeli, adórant Dominatiónes, tremunt Potestátes. Cæli cælorúmque Virtútes ac beáta Séraphim sócia exsultatióne concélebrant. Cum quibus et nostras voces, ut admítti, iúbeas, deprecámur, súpplici conféssione dicéntes:

It is truly right and just, our duty and our salvation, always and everywhere to give thee thanks, Lord, holy Father, almighty and eternal God: through Christ our Lord. Through him the Angels praise your majesty, Dominions adore and Powers tremble before you. Heaven and the Virtues of heaven and the blessed Seraphim worship together in exultation. May our voices, we pray, join with theirs in humble praise as we acclaim:

## Preface of the Blessed Virgin Mary

Vere dignum et iustum est, æquum et salutáre, nos tibi semper et ubíque grátias ágere: Dómine, sancte Pater, omnípotens ætérne Deus: Et te in [Veneratióne, *vel* Festivitáte *etc.*] beátæ Maríæ semper Vírginis collaudáre, benedícere et prædicáre. Quæ et Unigénitum tuum Sancti Spíritus obumbratióne concépit: et, virginitátis glória permanénte, lumen ætérnum mundo effúdit, Iesum Christum, Dóminum nostrum. Per quem maiestátem tuam laudant Angeli, adórant Dominatiónes, tremunt Potestátes. Cæli cælorúmque Virtútes ac beáta Séraphim sócia exsultatióne concélebrant. Cum quibus et nostras voces ut admítti iúbeas, deprecámur, súpplici confessióne dicéntes:

It is truly right and just, our duty and our salvation, always and everywhere to give thee thanks, Lord, holy Father, almighty and eternal God, and to praise, bless, and glorify thy name in [veneration *or* the festival *etc.*] of the Blessed evervirgin Mary. For by the overshadowing of the Holy Ghost she conceived thy Only Begotten Son, and, without losing the glory of virginity, brought forth into the world the eternal Light, Jesus Christ our Lord. Through him the Angels praise thy majesty, Dominions adore and Powers tremble before thee. Heaven and the Virtues of heaven and the blessed Seraphim worship together with exultation. May our voices, we pray, join with theirs in humble praise as we acclaim:

# Preface of Lent

Vere dignum et iustum est, æquum et salutáre, nos tibi semper, et ubíque grátias agere: Dómine, sancte Pater, omnípotens ætérne Deus: Qui corporáli ieiúnio vítia cómprimis, mentem élevas, virtútem largíris et præmia : per Christum Dóminum nostrum. Per quem maiestátem tuam laudant Angeli, adórant Dominatiónes, tremunt Potestátes. Cæli cælorúmque Virtútes, ac beáta Séraphim, sócia exsultatióne concélebrant. Cum quibus et nostras voces, ut admitti iúbeas, deprecámur, súpplici confessióne dicentes:

It is truly right and just, our duty and our salvation, always and everywhere to give thee thanks, Lord, holy Father, almighty and eternal God. For through bodily fasting thou dost restrain our faults, raise up our minds, and bestow both virtue and its rewards, through Christ our Lord. Through him the Angels praise thy majesty, Dominions adore and Powers tremble before thee. Heaven and the Virtues of heaven and the blessed Seraphim worship together in exultation. May our voices, we pray, join with theirs in humble praise as we acclaim:

# Preface of Easter and Paschaltide

Vere dignum et iustum est, æquum et salutáre, te quidem, Dómine, omni témpore, sed [in hac potíssimum nocte, *vel* in hac potíssimum die, *vel* in hoc potíssimum] gloriósius prædícare, cum Pascha nostrum immolátus est Christus. Ipse enim verus est Agnus, qui ábstulit peccáta mundi. Qui mortem nostram moriéndo destrúxit et vitam resurgéndo reparávit. Et ídeo cum Angelis et Archángelis, cum Thronis et Dominatiónibus cumque omni milítia cæléstis exércitus, hymnum glóriæ tuæ cánimus, sine fine dicéntes:

It it truly right and just, our duty and our salvation, at all times to praise Thee, O Lord, but [on this night *or* on this day *or* in this time] above all to laud thee yet more gloriously, when Christ our Passover has been sacrificed. For he is the true Lamb who has taken away the sins of the world; by dying he has destroyed our death, and by rising, restored our life. And so, with Angels and Archangels, with Thrones and Dominions, and with all the hosts and Powers of heaven, we sing the hymn of thy glory, as without end we acclaim:

# Ritus Aspersionis

*Before the Principal Mass on Sundays*

*At the Principal Mass on Sundays the Priest processes in wearing a cope, and while the Asperges or Vidi Aquam is sung, he sprinkles the Faithful with Holy Water. When this is concluded, he goes into the Sanctuary and changes his cope for a chasuble.*

*The Chant settings are on p58–59.*

*Sacerdos:* Aspérges me
*Omnes:* Dómine, hyssópo, et mundábor: lavábis me, et super nivem dealbábor.
*Cantores:* Miserére mei, Deus,
*Omnes:* secúndum magnam misericórdiam tuam.
*Cantores:* Glória Patri, et Fílio, et Spirítui Sancto,

*Omnes:* Sicut erat in princípio, et nunc, et semper, et in sǽcula sæculórum. Amen. Aspérges me…

*S:* Osténde nobis, Dómine, misericórdiam tuam.
*R:* Et salutáre tuum da nobis.
*S:* Dómine, exáudi oratiónem meam.
*R:* Et clamor meus ad te véniat.
*S:* Dóminus vobíscum.
*R:* Et cum spíritu tuo.

*S:* Oremus.
Exáudi nos, Dómine, sancte Pater, omnípotens ætérne Deus: et míttere dignéris sanctum Ángelum tuum de cælis, qui custódiat, fóveat, prótegat, vísitet, atque deféndat omnes habitántes in hoc habitáculo. Per Christum Dóminum nostrum.
*R:* Amen.

*During Eastertide the Antiphon and Verse are as follows:*

*Sacerdos*: Vidi aquam
*Omnes:* egrediéntem de templo, a látere dextro, allelúia: et omnes ad quos pervénit aqua ista salvi facti sunt, et dicent: allelúia, allelúia.
*Cantores*: Confitémini Dómino, quóniam bonus;
*Omnes:* quóniam in sǽculum misericórdia eius.
*Cantores*: Glória Patri… [*dialogue follows as above*]

# Asperges *or* Vidi Aquam

*at the beginning of the Principal Mass on Sundays*

*Priest:* Thou shalt sprinkle me
*All:* With hyssop, O Lord, and I shall be cleansed; thou shalt wash me, and I shall be made whiter than snow.
*Cantors:* Have mercy on me, O God,
*All:* according to thy great mercy.
*Cantors:* Glory be to the Father and to the Son and to the Holy Ghost.
*All:* As it was in the beginning, is now, and ever shall be, world without end. Amen. Thou shalt sprinkle me...

*P:* Show us, O Lord, thy mercy.
*R:* And grant us thy salvation.
*P:* Lord, hear my prayer.
*R:* And let my cry come unto thee.
*P:* The Lord be with you.
*R:* And with thy spirit.

*P:* Let us pray.
Graciously hear us, Lord, holy Father, almighty and eternal God; and be pleased to send thy holy Angel from heaven to watch over, to cherish, to protect, to abide with, and to defend all who dwell in this house. Through Christ our Lord.

*R:* Amen.

**Stand.**

**Make the sign of the cross when you are sprinkled.**

*During Eastertide the Antiphon and Verse are as follows:*

*Priest*: I saw water
*All:* flowing from the right side of the Temple, alleluia: and all to whom that water came were saved, and they shall say: alleluia, alleluia.
*Cantors*: Give praise to the Lord, for he is good,
*All:* for his mercy endures forever.
*Cantors*: Glory be... [*dialogue follows as above*]

# Prayers for Communion

*These prayers are taken from the Roman Missal.*

### Prayer of St Thomas Aquinas before Communion

Omnípotens sempitérne Deus, ecce, accédo ad sacraméntum unigéniti Fílii tui, Dómini nostri Iesu Christi; accédo tamquam infírmus ad médicum vitæ, immúndus ad fontem misericórdiæ, cæcus ad lumen claritátis ætérnæ, pauper et egénus ad Dóminum cæli et terræ. Rogo ergo imménsæ largitátis tuæ abundántiam, quaténus meam curáre dignéris infirmitátem, laváre fœditátem, illumináre cæcitátem, ditáre paupertátem, vestire nuditátem; ut panem Angelórum, Regem regum et Dóminum domynántium, tanta suscípiam reveréntia et humilitáte, tanta contritióne et devotióne, tanta puritáte et fide, tali propósito et intentióne, sicut expédit salúti ánimæ meæ. Da mihi, quæso, Domínici Córporis et Sánguinis non solum suscípere sacraméntum, sed étiam rem et virtútem sacraménti. O mitíssime Deus, da mihi Corpus unigéniti Fílii tui, Dómini nostri Iesu Christi, quod traxit de Vírgine María, sic suscípere, ut córpori suo mýstico mérear incorporári, et inter eius membra connumerári. O amantíssime Pater, concéde mihi diléctum Fílium tuum, quem

Almighty and eternal God, behold, I approach the sacrament of thy only-begotten Son, our Lord Jesus Christ. I approach as one who is sick to the physician of life, as one unclean to the fountain of mercy, as one blind to the light of eternal brightness, as one poor and needy to the Lord of heaven and earth. Therefore I beseech thee, of thy boundless generosity: be pleased to heal my sickness, to wash away my filth, to enlighten my blindness, to enrich my poverty, and to clothe my nakedness, that I may receive the Bread of angels, the King of kings and Lord of lords with such reverence and humility, with such contrition and devotion, with such purity and faith, with such purpose and intention, as may further the salvation of my soul. Grant, I beseech thee, that I may receive not only the sacrament of the Body and Blood of our Lord, but also the reality and power of the sacrament. O most gentle God, grant me so to receive the Body of thy only-begotten Son, our Lord Jesus Christ, which he took of the Virgin Mary, that I may be found fit to be incorporated with his mystical body and numbered among his limbs. O most loving Father, grant that I may one day contemplate unceasingly with his face revealed thy

nunc velátum in via suscípere propóno, reveláta tandem fácie perpétuo contemplári: Qui tecum vivit et regnat in unitáte Spíritus Sancti Deus: per ómnia sǽcula sæculórum. Amen.

beloved Son, whom now, a wayfarer, I resolve to receive under a veil; who lives and reigns with thee in the unity of the Holy Ghost, God, for ever and ever. Amen.

## Prayer after Communion

Grátias tibi ago, Dómine, sancte Pater, omnípotens, ætérne Deus, qui me peccatórem, indígnum fámulum tuum, nullis meis méritis, sed sola dignatióne misericórdiæ tuæ satiáre dignátus es pretióso Córpore et Sánguine Filii tui, Dómini nostri Iesu Christi. Et precor, ut hæc sancta commúnio non sit mihi reátus ad pœnam, sed intercéssio salutáris ad véniam. Sit mihi armatúra fídei et scutum bonæ voluntátis. Sit vitiórum meórum evacuátio, concupiscéntiæ et libídinis exterminátio, caritátis et patiéntiæ, humilitátis et obœdiéntiæ, omniúmque virtútum augmentátio: contra insídias inimicórum ómnium, tam visibílium quam invisibílium, firma defénsio: mótuum meórum, tam carnálium quam spirituálium, perfécta quietátio: in te uno ac vero Deo firma adhǽsio; atque finis mei felix consummátio. Et precor te, ut ad illud ineffábile convívium me peccatórem perdúcere dignéris, ubi tu cum Fílio tuo et Spíritu Sancto Sanctis tuis es lux vera, satíetas

I give thee thanks, Lord, holy Father, almighty and eternal God, who hast been pleased, not for any merits of mine, but only out of the condescension of thy mercy, to satisfy me a sinner, thy unworthy servant, with the precious Body and Blood of thy Son our Lord Jesus Christ. And I pray that this holy communion be not to me a condemnation to punishment, but a saving plea to forgiveness. May it be to me the armour of faith and the shield of a good will. May it be the emptying out of my vices, the extinction of all concupiscence and lust, the increase of charity and patience, of humility and obedience, and of all virtues; a strong defence against the snares of all enemies, visible and invisible; the quieting of all my evil impulses, both carnal and spiritual; a firm cleaving to thee, the one true God; and the happy accomplishment of my destiny. And I pray thee, that thou wouldst be pleased to bring me, a sinner, to that banquet, wonderful past all telling, where thou, with thy Son and the Holy Ghost,

plena, gáudium sempitérnum, iucúnditas consummáta et felícitas perfécta. Per eúndem Christum, Dóminum nostrum. Amen.

art to thy Saints true light, total fulfilment, eternal joy, unalloyed gladness and perfect happiness. Through the same Christ our Lord. Amen.

## Anima Christi

Anima Christi, sanctífica me.
Corpus Christi, salva me.
Sanguis Christi, inébria me.
Aqua láteris Christi, lava me.

Soul of Christ, sanctify me.
Body of Christ, save me.
Blood of Christ, inebriate me.
Water from the side of Christ, wash me.

Pássio Christi, confórta me.
O bone Iesu, exáudi me.
Intra tua vúlnera abscónde me.
Ne permíttas me separári a te.

Passion of Christ, strengthen me.
O good Jesu, hear me.
Within thy wounds hide me.
Let me not to be separated from thee.

Ab hoste malígno defénde me.
In hora mortis meæ voca me.
Et iube me veníre ad te,
Ut cum Sanctis tuis laudem te
In sǽcula sæculórum. Amen.

From the malicious enemy defend me.
In the hour of my death call me,
And bid me come unto thee,
that with thy Saints I may praise thee
for ever and ever. Amen.

## Obsecro Te

Obsécro te, dulcíssime Dómine Iesu Christe, ut pássio tua sit mihi virtus, qua múniar, prótegar atque deféndar; vúlnera tua sint mihi cibus potúsque, quibus pascar, inébrier atque delécter; aspérsio Sánguinis tui sit mihi ablútio ómnium delictórum meórum: mors tua sit mihi vita indefíciens, Crux tua sit mihi glória sempitérna. In

I entreat thee, most sweet Lord Jesus Christ, grant that thy Passion may be to me a power by which I may be strengthened, protected and defended. May thy wounds be to me food and drink, by which I may be nourished, inebriated and overjoyed. May the sprinkling of thy Blood be to me the washing away of all my offences. May thy death be to me never

his sit mihi reféctio, exsultátio, sánitas et dulcédo cordis mei: Qui vivis et regnas in sǽcula sæculórum. Amen.

failing life, and thy Cross be my everlasting glory. In these may there be my heart's renewal, gladness, health and sweetness: who livest and reignest for ever and ever. Amen.

## Prayer before a Crucifix

En ego, o bone et dulcíssime Iesu, ante conspéctum tuum génibus me provólvo ac máximo ánimi ardóre te oro atque obtéstor, ut meum in cor vívidos fídei, spei et caritátis sensus, atque veram peccatórum meórum pæniténtiam, éaque emendándi firmíssimam voluntátem velis imprímere; dum magno animi afféctu et dolóre tua quinque vúlnera mecum ipse

Behold, O kind and most sweet Jesus, I cast myself upon my knees in thy sight, and with the most fervent desire of my soul, I pray and beseech thee that thou wouldst impress upon my heart lively sentiments of faith, hope and charity, with true contrition for my sins and a firm purpose of amendment; while with deep affection and grief of mind I ponder within myself and mentally

consídero ac mente contémplor, illud præ óculis habens, quod iam in ore ponébat tuo David Prophéta de te, o bone Iesu: "Fodérunt manus meas et pedes meos; dinumeravérunt ómnia ossa mea." (Ps. 21:17–18).

contemplate thy five wounds, having before my eyes the words which David the prophet put on thy lips concerning thee: "They have dug my hands and my feet, they have numbered all my bones" (Ps. 21:17–18).

# Ad Benedictionem SS. Sacramenti

*Hymn, 'O Salutaris'*

*The hymn is sung as soon as the priest enters, and while he exposes the Blessed Sacrament in the monstrance.*

O Salutáris Hóstia
Quæ cæli pandis óstium
Bella premunt hostília;
Da robur, fer auxílium.

Uni trinóque Dómino,
Sit sempitérna glória;
Qui vitam sine término,
Nobis donet in pátria. Amen.

*The Litany of Loreto (p69) may be sung at this point, or other prayers said.*

### Prayer for England

*On the 2nd Sunday of the month the longer Prayer for England is used: see p71.*

O beáta Virgo María, Mater Dei, Regína nostra et Mater dulcíssima, benígna óculos tuos convérte ad Angliam, quæ Dos tua vocátur, convérte ad nos, qui magna in te fidúcia confídimus.

Per te datus est Christus Salvátor mundi, in quo spes nostra consísteret; ab ipso autem tu data es nobis, per quam spes éadem augeretur. Eia ígitur, ora pro nobis, quos tibi apud Crucem Dómini excepísti fílios, o pérdolens Mater: intercéde pro frátribus dissidéntibus, ut nobíscum in único vero Ovíli adiungántur summo Pastóri, Vicário in terris Fílii tui.

Pro nobis ómnibus deprecáre, o Mater piíssima, ut per fidem, bonis opéribus fecúndam, mereámur tecum omnes contemplári Deum in cælésti pátria et collaudáre per sǽcula.

℟. Amen.

# Benediction of the Blessed Sacrament

O Saving Victim, thou who dost throw open heaven's gate, the enemy's wars press hard on us; give us strength, bring us help.

Everlasting glory be to the Lord, one and three; and may he give us unending life in our Father's land. Amen.

*As the priest enters, kneel.*

*This translation of the O Salutaris is by Fr Joseph Connelly*

*Turn the page for the Prayers for Wales and Scotland.*

### PRAYER FOR ENGLAND

O Blessed Virgin Mary, Mother of God and our most gentle Queen and Mother, look down in mercy upon England, thy dowry, and upon us who greatly hope and trust in thee.

By thee it was that Jesus, our Saviour and our hope was given unto the world; and he has given thee to us that we might hope still more.

Plead for us thy children, whom thou didst receive and accept at the foot of the Cross, O sorrowful Mother! Intercede for our separated brethren, that with us in the one true fold they may be united to the chief Shepherd, the Vicar of thy Son.

Pray for us all, dear Mother, that by faith fruitful in good works we may all deserve to see and praise God, together with thee, in our heavenly home.

℟. Amen.

The Prayer for England is usually said in English.

*The prayer was promulgated by Pope Leo XIII in 1895.*

## GWEDDI DROS GYMRU

*The Prayer for Wales may be said, in Wales, in the Welsh language.*

*This version was author-ised by Arch-bishop McGrath of Cardiff in 1949.*

O Hollalluog Dduw a ddanfonodd, o'th anfeidrol ddaioni, dy uniganedig Fab i ailagor porth y nefoedd, ac i ddysgu inni dy adnabod, dy garu a'th wasnaethu, trugarha wrth dy bobl sy'n byw yng Nghymru. Dyro iddynt y werthfawr ddawn Ffydd, ac una hwy yn yr un wir Eglwys a sylfaenwyd gan dy ddwyfol Fab, fel, gan arddel ei hawdurdod a chan ufuddhau i'w llais, y'th wasnaethont Di, a'th garu a'th addoli yn ôl dy ewyllys yn y byd hwn, ac felly dderbyn ohonynt dded-wyddwch tragwyddol yn y byd a ddaw. Trwy'r un Iesu Grist ein Harglwydd.

R̃. Amen.

Ṽ. Ein Harglwyddes, Gymorth Cristnogion,

R̃. gweddïa dros Gymru.

Ṽ. Dewi Sant,

R̃. gweddïa dros Gymru.

Ṽ. Santes Wenfrewi,

R̃. gweddïa dros Gymru.

Ṽ. Holl Santiau Gymru,

R̃. Gweddïwch dros Gymru.

## PRAYER FOR SCOTLAND

O blessed St Andrew, First-Called and Fisher of men, of old thou didst summon thy brother St Peter into the presence of the Saviour; obtain now, we beseech thee, by thy powerful intercession for the people of Scot-land that they might recognise in his successor the Vicar of Christ, and so enter into the vision of him who with the Father and the Holy Ghost lives and reigns, one God, for ever and ever. Amen.

### PRAYER FOR WALES

O Almighty God, who in thy infinite goodness hast sent thy only-begotten Son into this world to open once more the gates of heaven, and to teach us how to know, love and serve thee, have mercy on thy people who dwell in Wales. Grant to them the precious gift of faith, and unite them in the one true Church founded by thy divine Son; that, acknowledging her authority and obeying her voice, they may serve thee, love thee, and worship thee as thou desirest in this world, and obtain for themselves everlasting happiness in the world to come. Through the same Christ our Lord.

℟. Amen.

℣. Our Lady, Help of Christians,

℟. pray for Wales.

℣. Saint David,

℟. pray for Wales.

℣. Saint Winefride,

℟. pray for Wales.

℣. All the saints of Wales,

℟. pray for Wales.

### PRAYER FOR SCOTLAND

O blessed St Andrew, First-Called and Fisher of men, of old thou didst summon thy brother St Peter into the presence of the Saviour; obtain now, we beseech thee, by thy powerful intercession for the people of Scotland that they might recognise in his successor the Vicar of Christ, and so enter into the vision of him who with the Father and the Holy Ghost lives and reigns, one God, for ever and ever. Amen.

*The Tantum ergo is then sung.*

Tantum ergo sacraméntum,
Venerémur cérnui;
Et antíquum documéntum
Novo cedat rítui;
Præstet fides suppleméntum
Sénsuum deféctui.

Genitóri, Genitóque,
Laus et iubilátio
Salus, honor, virtus quoque
Sit et benedíctio
Procedénti ab utróque
Compar sit laudátio. Amen.

*'Alleluia' is added during Paschaltide and on Corpus Christi.*

℣. Panem de cælo præstitísti eis (Allelúia).
℟. Omne delectaméntum in se habéntem (Allelúia).

℣. Orémus: Deus, qui nobis, sub sacraménto mirábili, passiónis tuæ memóriam reliquísti, tríbue quǽsumus, ita nos córporis et sánguinis tui sacra mystéria venerári, ut redemptiónis tui fructum in nobis iúgiter sentiámus. Qui vivis et regnas in sǽcula sæculórum.

℟. Amen.

Parce, Dómine, parce pópulo tuo, et ne in ætérnum irascáris nobis. *(Ter)*

*The Priest, wearing the Humeral Veil, blesses the Faithful with the Blessed Sacrament.*

Let us therefore humbly reverence so great a sacrament. Let the old types depart and give way to the new rite. Let faith provide her help where all the senses fail.

*This translation of the Tantum ergo is by Fr Joseph Connelly.*

To the Father and the Son be praise, acclamation, salutation, honour, might and blessing too. To the One who proceeds from them both be given equal praise. Amen

℣. Thou hast given them bread from heaven (Alleluia).
℟. Having in it all that is delicious (Alleluia).

℣. Let us pray: O God, who in this wonderful Sacrament hast left us a memorial of thy passion: grant us, we pray, so to revere the sacred mysteries of thy Body and Blood, that we may always experience in ourselves the fruit of thy redemption. Who livest and reignest forever and ever.

℟. Amen.

*This invocation 'may always be recited or sung' here (Manual of Prayers).*

> Spare, O Lord, spare thy people, and be not angry with them for ever. (*Thrice*)

*The Priest, wearing the Humeral Veil, blesses the Faithful with the Blessed Sacrament.*

*The Divine Praises*

Benedíctus Deus.
Benedíctum Nomen Sanctum eius.
Benedíctus Iesus Christus, verus Deus et verus homo.
Benedíctum Nomen Iesu.
Benedíctum Cor eius sacratíssimum.
Benedíctus Sanguis eius pretiosíssimus.
Benedíctus Iesus in sanctíssimo altáris Sa, Sacraménto.

Benedíctus Sanctus Spíritus, Paráclitus.
Benedícta magna Mater Dei, María sanctíssima.
Benedícta sancta eius et immaculáta Concéptio.
Benedícta gloriósa eius Assúmptio.
Benedíctum nomen Maríæ, Vírginis et Matris.
Benedíctus sanctus Ioseph, eius castíssimus Sponsus.
Benedíctus Deus in Angelis suis et in Sanctis suis.

*Antiphon*: Adorémus in ætérnum sanctíssimum Sacra-méntum.

Laudáte Dóminum omnes gentes: laudáte eum omnes pópuli.
Quóniam confirmáta est super nos misericórdia eius: et véritas Dómini manet in ætérnum.

*'Adoremus in æternum'*

*Ant:* Adorémus in ætérnum sanctíssimum Sacraméntum.

Glória Patri, et Fílio, et Spirítui Sancto: Sicut erat in princípio, et nunc et semper, et in sǽcula sæculórum. Amen.

*Ant:* Adorémus in ætérnum sanctíssimum Sacraméntum.

*A Marian Anthem may follow, according to the season:*

54

Blessed be God.

Blessed be his holy Name.

Blessed be Jesus Christ, true God and true man.

Blessed be the name of Jesus.

Blessed be his most sacred Heart.

Blessed be his most precious Blood.

Blessed be Jesus in the most holy Sacrament of the Altar.

Blessed be the Holy Ghost, the Paraclete.

Blessed be the great Mother of God, Mary most holy.

Blessed be her holy and immaculate Conception.

Blessed be her glorious Assumption.

Blessed be the name of Mary, virgin and mother.

Blessed be St Joseph, her spouse most chaste.

Blessed be God in his Angels and in his Saints.

*Antiphon:* Let us adore for ever the most holy Sacrament.

*While the Antiphon and Psalm 116 are sung, the priest returns to the altar and removes the Blessed Sacrament from the monstrance, replaces it in the tabernacle, then returns to the foot of the altar.*

Praise the Lord, all ye nations: praise him all ye peoples.

Because his mercy is confirmed upon us: and the truth of the Lord remains forever.

*Ant:* Let us adore for ever the most holy Sacrament.

Glory be to the Father, and to the Son, and to the Holy Ghost: as it was in the beginning, is now, and ever shall be, world without end. Amen.

*Ant:* Let us adore for ever the most holy Sacrament.

# Salutatio Angelica

℣. Angelus Dómini nuntiávit Maríæ.

℟. Et concépit de Spíritu Sancto.

Omnes: Ave María, grátia plena, Dóminus tecum, benedícta tu in muliéribus, et benedíctus fructus ventris tui Iesus. Sancta María, Mater Dei, ora pro nobis peccatóribus, nunc et in hora mortis nostræ. Amen.

℣. Ecce ancílla Dómini.

℟. Fiat mihi secúndum verbum tuum.

    Ave María...

℣. Et Verbum caro factum est. (*kneel*)

℟. Et habitávit in nobis. *(stand)*

    Ave María...

℣. Ora pro nobis, Sancta Dei Génetrix.

℟. Ut digni efficiámur promissiónibus Christi.

℣. Orémus. Grátiam tuam, quæsumus, Dómine, méntibus nostris infúnde; ut qui, Angelo nuntiánte, Christi Fílii tui incarnatiónem cognóvimus, per passiónem eius et crucem, ad resurrectiónis glóriam perducámur. Per eúndem Christum Dóminum nostrum.

℟. Amen.

## Antiphona Mariana (*tempore Paschale*)

Omnes: Regína cæli, lætáre, allelúia: Quia quem meruísti portáre, allelúia,   Resurréxit sicut dixit, allelúia: Ora pro nobis Deum, allelúia.

℣. Gaude et lætáre, Virgo Maria, allelúia,

℟. Quia surréxit Dóminus vere, allelúia.

℣. Orémus. Deus, qui per resurrectiónem Fílii tui Dómini nostri Iesu Christi, mundum lætificáre dignátus es: præsta, quæsumus, ut per eius Genetrícem Vírginem Maríam perpétuæ capiámus gaudia vitæ. Per eúndem Christum Dóminum nostrum.

℟. Amen.

# The Angelus

℣. The Angel of the Lord declared unto Mary:

℟. And she conceived by the Holy Ghost.

All: Hail Mary, full of grace, the Lord is with thee; blessed art thou amongst women and blessed is the fruit of thy womb, Jesus. Holy Mary, Mother of God, pray for us sinners, now and at the hour of our death. Amen.

℣. Behold the handmaid of the Lord:

℟. Be it done unto me according to thy word.

> Hail Mary . . .

℣. And the Word was made flesh: (*kneel*)

℟. And dwelt amongst us. (*stand*)

> Hail Mary . . .

℣. Pray for us, O Holy Mother of God,

℟. That we may be made worthy of the promises of Christ.

℣. Let us pray: Pour forth, we beseech thee, O Lord, thy grace into our hearts; that we, to whom the incarnation of Christ thy Son was made known by the message of an angel, may by his Passion and Cross be brought to the glory of his Resurrection, through the same Christ Our Lord.

℟. Amen.

## Regina Cæli (*during Paschaltide*)

All: Queen of Heaven rejoice, alleluia: For he whom thou wast worthy to bear, alleluia, Has risen as he said, alleluia: Pray for us to God, alleluia.

℣. Rejoice and be glad, O Virgin Mary, alleluia.

℟. Because the Lord is truly risen, alleluia.

℣. Let us pray. O God, who by the resurrection of thy Son, our Lord Jesus Christ, wast pleased to give joy to the world: grant we beseech thee, that through his Mother the Virgin Mary we may obtain the joys of eternal life. Through the same Christ our Lord.

℟. Amen.

# CHANTS FOR THE MASS

## Asperges

*sung at the beginning of Mass, on the principal Sung Mass on a Sunday, except during Eastertide.*

-spérges me, * Dómi-ne, hyssó-po, et mundá-bor: lavá-bis me, et super nivem de- albá- bor. *Ps.50.* Mi- se-rére me-i, De- us, * se-cúndum magnam mise-ricórdi- am tu- am. Gló- ri- a Patri, et Fí-li- o, et Spi-rí-tu-i Sancto: * Sic-ut e-rat in princí-pi-o, et nunc, et semper, et in saécula saecu-lórum. A- men.

*Repeat Ant.* Asperges me.

¶ *On the first Sunday of the Passion the* Glória Patri. *is not said, but the Antiphon* Asperges me. *is repeated immediately after the Psalm.*
*On the Second Sunday of the Passion or Palm Sunday, the* Asperges *is omitted.*

℣. Osténde nobis, Dómine, misericórdiam tuam.
℟. Et salutáre tuum da nobis.
℣. Dómine, exáudi oratiónem meam.
℟. Et clamor meus ad te véniat.

℣. Dóminus vobíscum.
℟. Et cum spíritu tuo.
℣. Orémus. …. Per Christum Dóminum nostrum.
℟. Amen.

# Vidi Aquam

*Sung in place of the Asperges during Eastertide.*

Ant. VIII. X. s.

Vidi a-quam * egre- di- éntem de tem-plo a lá-tere dex- tro, alle- lú- ia : et omnes, ad quos pervénit a-qua i-sta sal- vi fa- cti sunt, et di- cent: alle-lú- ia, al- le- lú- ia. *Ps.117* Confi- témini Dómino, quó-ni- am bonus : * quó-ni- am in saéculum mise-ricór- di- a ejus. Glóri- a Patri, et Fí-li-o, et Spirí- tu-i Sancto: *Sic-ut erat in princí-pi-o, et nunc, et semper, et in saécula saecu- ló-rum. Amen.

*Repeat Ant. Vidi aquam.*

℣. Osténde nobis, Dómine, misericórdiam tuam, allelúia.
℟. Et salutáre tuam da nobis, allelúia.
℣. Dómine, exáudi oratiónem meam.
℟. Et clamor meus ad te véniat.

℣. Dóminus vobíscum.
℟. Et cum spíritu tuo.
℣. Orémus. …. Per Christum Dóminum nostrum.
℟. Amen.

## XI. IN DOMINICIS INFRA ANNUM
( Orbis factor )

**(X) XIV-XVI. s.**

I.

Ký-ri- e * e- lé- i-son. *iij.* Chri-ste e- lé- i-

son. *iij.* Kýri- e e- lé-i-son. *ij.* Ký- ri- e * e-

lé- i-son.

**X. s.**

II.

Gló-ri- a in excélsis De- o. Et in terra pax homíni- bus

bonæ voluntá-tis. **Laudámus te.** Benedí- cimus te. **Adorámus**

te. Glo-ri-fi-cámus te. **Gráti- as ágimus ti-bi propter**

**magnam gló-ri- am tu- am.** Dómi- ne De- us, Rex cæ-léstis, De-

us, Pater omní-potens. **Dómi-ne Fi- li uni-géni-te, Ie- su**

**Christe.** Domi-ne De- us, Agnus De- i, Fí- li-us Patris. **Qui tol-**

lis peccáta mundi, mise-rére nobis. Qui tollis peccá-ta mun-

di, súscipe depreca-ti- onem nostram. **Qui sedes ad déxteram**

**Patris, mise-rére nobis.** Quóni- am tu solus Sanctus. **Tu so-**

lus Dóminus. Tu so-lus Altíssimus Ie-su Christe. **Cum San-**

cto Spí-ritu, in glóri- a De- i Pa- tris. A-men.

XI. s.

II.

anctus, * San-ctus, Sanctus, Dóminus De- us Sá-ba-oth.

Pleni sunt cæ- li et ter- ra gló-ri- a tu-a. Hosánna in ex-

célsis. Benedíctus qui ve-nit in nó-mine Dó-mini. Hosán-

na in ex- célsis.

XIV. s.

I.

A-gnus De-i, * qui tollis peccá-ta mundi: miseré-re nobis.

Agnus De-i, * qui tol-lis peccáta mundi : miseré-re nobis.

Agnus De-i, * qui tollis peccá- ta mundi : dona nobis pacem.

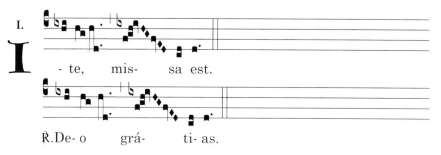

I.

- te, mis- sa est.

℟.De- o grá- ti- as.

## XVII. IN DOMINICIS ADVENTUS ET QUADRAGESIMAE

XIV. s.

VI.

Ký-ri- e * e- lé- i-son. *iij.* Christe e- lé- i-son.

*iij.*Ký-ri- e e- lé- i-son. *ij.*Ký-ri- e * e-

lé- i-son.

**V.** San-ctus, * Sanctus, San-ctus, Dóminus De- us Sá- ba- oth.

Ple-ni sunt cæ- li et ter-ra glóri- a tu- a. Ho- sánna in

excél- sis. Bene-díctus, qui venit in nó-mine Dómi-ni. Ho- sán-

na in excél- sis.

**V.** -gnus De- i, * qui tol-lis peccá-ta mundi : mise-rére no-

bis Agnus De- i, * qui tol-lis peccá-ta mundi : miseré-re no-bis

Agnus De- i, * qui tol-lis peccá-ta mundi : dona nobis pa- cem.

**IV.** - te, mis-sa est. ℟. De- o grá- ti- as.

# CREDO I

**IV.**

**C**redo *in unum De-um,* Patrem omnipot-éntem, factórem

cæ-li et terræ, vi-si-bí-li- um ómni-um, et invi-si-bíli- um. **Et in**

**unum Dóminum  Iesum Christum, Fíli- um De-i  uni-géni-**

**tum.** Et ex Patre natum  ante ómni- a sǽcu-la.  **De-um de De-**

**o,  lumen de lúmine,  De-um verum de De-o vero.** Gé-ni-

tum, non factum, consubstanti- á-lem Patri :  per quem ómni- a

facta sunt. **Qui propter nos hómines,  et propter nostram**

**salútem descéndit de cæ-lis.** Et incarnátus est de Spí-ri-tu

Sancto  ex Marí- a Vírgi- ne :  Et homo factus est. **Cruci-fí-xus**

**ét-i- am pro nobis: sub Pónti-o Pi-láto  passus et sepúltus**

64

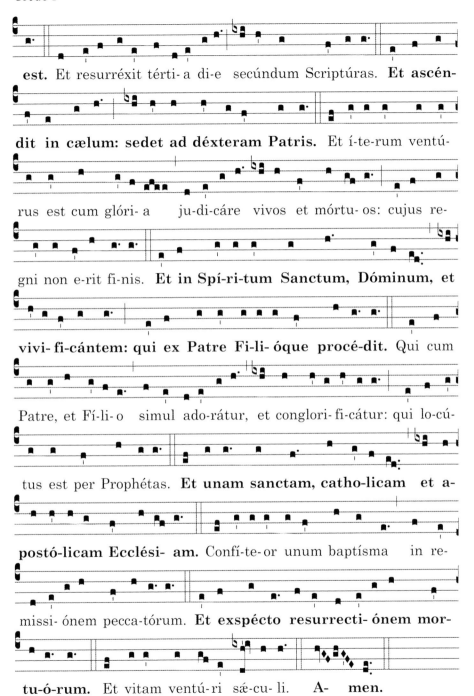

est. Et resurréxit térti- a di-e secúndum Scriptúras. **Et ascén-**

**dit in cælum: sedet ad déxteram Patris.** Et í-te-rum ventú-

rus est cum glóri- a ju-di-cáre vivos et mórtu- os: cujus re-

gni non e-rit fi-nis. **Et in Spí-ri-tum Sanctum, Dóminum, et**

**vivi- fi-cántem: qui ex Patre Fi-li- óque procé-dit.** Qui cum

Patre, et Fí-li- o simul ado-rátur, et conglori- fi-cátur: qui lo-cú-

tus est per Prophétas. **Et unam sanctam, catho-licam et a-**

**postó-licam Ecclési- am.** Confí-te- or unum baptísma in re-

missi- ónem pecca-tórum. **Et exspécto resurrecti- ónem mor-**

tu-ó-rum. Et vitam ventú-ri sǽ-cu- li. A- men.

# Marian Anthems (Simple Tones)

*From Vespers before the First Sunday of Advent
until the Compline before the Purification (2nd Feb).*

Alma * Redemptóris, Mater, quae pérvi-a cæ-li porta ma-
nes, Et stella maris, succúrre cadénti súrgere qui curat pópulo :
Tu quæ genu-ísti, natúra mi-ránte, tu-um sanctum Geni-tórem:
Virgo pri-us ac postéri-us, Gabri-é-lis ab ore sumens illud
Ave peccató-rum mi-se-ré-re.

*During Advent:*

℣. Ángelus Dómini nuntiávit Maríæ.

℟. Et concépit de Spíritu Sancto.

*From 1st Vespers of Christmas to 2nd Vespers of the Purification:*

℣. Post pártum Virgo invioláta permansísti.

℟. Dei Génetrix, intercéde pro nobis.

# Alma Redemptoris Mater, Ave Regina Cælorum & Regina Cæli

*From Compline before the Purification until Holy Week.*

VI.

-ve, Regína cæ-lórum, * Ave, Dómina Ange-lórum: Salve,

radix, salve, porta  Ex qua mundo lux est orta: Gaude, Virgo

glori- ósa, Su-per omnes spe-ci- ósa : Vale, o valde decó- ra,  Et

pro  nobis  Christum exó- ra.

℣. Dignáre me laudáre te, Virgo sacráta.

℟. Da míhi virtútem contra hóstes túos.

*From Compline of Holy Saturday until the Compline before Trinity Sunday.*

VI.

Egína cæ-li * lætáre, alle-lú-ia : Qui- a quem meru- ísti

portáre,  alle-lú-ia : Resurréxit, sic-ut dixit, alle-lú-ia : Ora pro

no-bis  De- um  alle-lú- ia :

℣. Gaude et  lætáre Virgo María, allelúia.

℟. Quia surréxit Dóminus vere, allelúia.

*From Compline before Trinity Sunday*
*until Vespers before the First Sunday of Advent.*

℣. Salve, Regína, * mater mi-se-ricórdi-æ : Vita, dulcé-do, et spes nóstra, salve. Ad te clamámus, éxsu-les, fí-li-i Hevæ. Ad te suspi-rámus, geméntes et flentes In hac lacrimárum valle. E-ia ergo, Advocáta nostra, illos tu-os mi-seri-córdes ócu-los ad nos convérte. Et Iesum, benedíctum fructum ventris tu-i, no-bis post hoc exsí-li-um osténde. O cle-mens: O pi- a: O dulcis Virgo Ma-rí- a.

℣. Ora pro nóbis sáncta Déi Génetrix.
℟. Ut dígni efficiámur promissiónibus Chrísti.

68

# LITANY OF LORETO
## in honour of the Blessed Virgin Mary

Kýri-e e-lé- i-son. *ij.* Christe e-lé- i-son. *ij.* Kýri- e e-lé-i-son. *ij.* Christe, audi nos. *ij.* Christe, exáudi nos. *ij.*

Pa- ter de *cœ*- lis De-us, * mi-se-rére nobis.
Fili Redémptor *mun*-di De-us, * mi-se-rére nobis.
Spí- ri- tus *Sancte* De-us, * mi-se-rére nobis.
Sancta Trínitas, *u*- nus De-us, * mi-se-rére nobis.

Sán-*cta* Ma-rí- a * ora pro nóbis.    *Má -* ter

Sáncta *Déi* **Génetrix**,
Sáncta *Vír*go **vírginum**,
*Má*ter **Chrísti**,
Má*ter* **Ecclésiæ**,
Máter Di*vín*æ **grátiæ**,
Má*ter* pu**ríss**ima,
Má*ter* cast**íss**ima,
Máter in*vi*o**láta**,
Máter in*te*mer**áta**,
Má*ter* am**áb**ilis,
Máter *ad*mir**ábilis**,
Máter bó*ni* cons**ílii**,
Máter *Crea***tóris**,
Máter *Salva***tóris**,
Vírgo *pru*den**tíss**ima,

Vírgo *vene***rán**da,
Vírgo *præ*di**cán**da,
*Vír*go **potens**,
*Vír*go **clemens**,
*Vír*go fi**délis**,
Spé*culum* iust**ítiæ**,
Sédes *sa*pi**éntiæ**,
Cáusa no*stræ* læ**títiæ**,
Vas spi*ritu***ále**,
Vas *hono***rábile**,
Vas insígne de*voti***ónis**,
*Ró*sa **mýstica**,
Túr*ris* Da**víd**ica,
Túr*ris* e**búr**nea,
*Dó*mus **áurea**,

69

Foéderis árca,
Iánua cǽli,
Stélla matutína,
Sálus infirmórum,
Refúgium peccatórum,
Consolátrix afflictórum,
Auxílium Christianórum,
Regína Angelórum,
Regína Patriarchárum,
Regína Prophetárum,
Regína Apostolórum,

Regína Mártyrum,
Regína Confessórum,
Regína Vírginum,
Regína Sanctórum ómnium,
Regína sine lábe origináli
   concépta,
Regína in cǽlum assúmpta,
Regína Sacratíssimi Rosárii,
Regína familiárum,
Regína pácis,

Agnus De-i, qui tollis peccáta mundi, * parce nobis, Dómine.

Agnus De-i, qui tollis peccáta mundi, * exáudi nos, Dómine.

Agnus De-i, qui tollis peccáta mundi, * mi-seré-re no-bis.

℣. Ora pro nobis, Sancta Dei Génetrix.

℟. Ut digni efficiámur promissiónibus Christi.

Orémus. Concéde nos fámulos tuos, quǽsumus, Dómine Deus, perpétua mentis et córporis sanitáte gaudére: et gloriósa beátæ Maríæ semper Vírginis intercessióne, a præsénti liberári tristítia, et ætérna pérfrui lætítia. Per Christum Dóminum nostrum.

℟. Amen.

## Long Prayer for England

*mandated by Cardinal Wiseman for Benediction on the Second Sundays.*

Hail Mary, etc.

O merciful God, let the glorious intercession of thy saints assist us; above all the most blessed Virgin Mary, Mother of thy only-begotten Son, and thy holy Apostles, Peter and Paul, to whose patronage we humbly recommend our land. Be mindful of our fathers, Eleutherius, Celestine and Gregory, bishops of the holy City; of Augustine, Columba, and Aidan, who delivered to us inviolate the faith of the holy Roman Church. Remember our holy martyrs, who shed their blood for Christ; especially our first martyr, Saint Alban, and thy most glorious bishop, Saint Thomas of Canterbury. Remember all those holy confessors, bishops and kings, all those holy monks and hermits, all those holy virgins and widows, who made this once an island of saints, illustrious by their glorious merits and virtues. Let not their memory perish from before thee, O Lord, but let their supplication enter daily into thy sight; and do thou, who didst so often spare thy sinful people for the sake of Abraham, Isaac and Jacob, now, also, moved by the prayers of our fathers, reigning with thee, have mercy upon us, save thy people, and bless thy inheritance; and suffer not those souls to perish, which thy Son has redeemed with his own most precious Blood. Who liveth and reigneth with thee, world without end.

R̄. Amen.

Let us pray. O loving Lord Jesus, who, when thou wert hanging on the Cross, didst commend us all, in the person of thy disciple John, to thy most sweet Mother, that we might find in her our refuge, our solace, and our hope; look graciously upon our beloved land, and on those who are bereaved of so powerful a patronage; that, acknowledging once more the dignity of this holy Virgin, they may honour and venerate her with all affection of devotion, and own her as Queen and Mother. May her sweet name be lisped by little ones, and linger on the lips of the aged and the dying; and may it be invoked by the afflicted, and hymned by the joyful; that this Star of the Sea being their protection and their guide, all may come to the harbour of eternal salvation. Who livest and reignest, world without end.

R̄. Amen.

# ABOUT THE LATIN MASS SOCIETY

The Latin Mass Society, founded in 1965, is an association of Catholic faithful dedicated to the promotion of the traditional Latin liturgy of the Catholic Church, the teachings and practices integral to it, the musical tradition which serves it, and the Latin language in which it is celebrated.

The intrinsic value and continuing importance of the Church's 'earlier liturgical traditions' have been affirmed by Pope Benedict XVI in his 2007 motu proprio *Summorum Pontificum*, which ruled that the Roman Missal of 1962—'the Missal of Pope Saint John XXIII'—has never been abrogated.

The Latin Mass Society organises Masses and devotional activities all over England and Wales; it organises training for both priests and laity in saying and serving Mass, in singing Gregorian Chant, and in Latin; it conducts and publishes research in related areas; and it represents the interests and concerns of the Faithful attached to the Church's liturgical traditions.

To this end we maintain a national network of Local Representatives, and a small paid staff.

To find out more and to join please visit our website or ring our London office: our contact details are on the back cover.

'It behoves all of us to preserve the riches which have developed in the Church's faith and prayer, and to give them their proper place.'

Pope Benedict XVI